A 1950s
IRISH
CHILDHOOD

A 1950s IRISH CHILDHOOD

From Catapults to Communion Medals

RUTH ILLINGWORTH

The History Press Ireland

This work is dedicated to all
the children of 1950s Ireland.

Front cover: Two boys at the O'Brien-Sheridan
Traveller Camp, May 1954. (National Library
of Ireland, Wiltshire Collection)

First published 2018

The History Press Ireland
50 City Quay
Dublin 2
Ireland
www.thehistorypress.ie

British Library Cataloguing in Publication Data.
A catalogue record for this book is available from the British Library.

ISBN 978 0 7509 8354 9

Typesetting and origination by The History Press
Printed and bound in Great Britain by TJ International Ltd

Contents

Introduction

Ireland in the 1950s was a very different country compared to the republic of today. In some ways it was closer to the Ireland of the Victorian era than to the twenty-first century. The children of the 1950s lived in a country that was still largely rural, deeply religious and poor. It was a country in which horse-drawn traps were still a common mode of transport in rural areas well into the decade, in which there were more cyclists than motorists, and many homes had no electric light or running water.

At the start of the decade, Ireland had been an independent state for just over a generation, and had become a republic and left the British Commonwealth only a year before. There was a strong sense of nationalism throughout the country and a sense of pride at the achievements of those who had fought for Irish independence between 1916 and 1921. The children of the 1950s were taught to revere the 1916 rebels, particularly the rebel leader Patrick Pearse, the poet and teacher, who was seen as a role model for the youth of Ireland. The continuing partition of the country was seen as a historical wrong and illegitimate. There was little understanding of the viewpoint of the Protestant Unionist majority in Northern Ireland. In the early part of the 1950s, the Irish government and opposition parties ran an international campaign against partition, and politicians called for Irish re-unification from election platforms. In the middle of the decade, the IRA began a military campaign, known as the Border Campaign, which would continue until 1962. Some teenagers would be drawn into that campaign having been exposed to extreme nationalist ideology in school and in the wider community.

The decade was one of political instability. There were three general elections in just six years and a succession of weak coalition or one-party minority administrations. Although there was a proliferation of small parties – such as Clann Na Poblachta, Clann Na Talmhan and Labour – the political scene remained dominated by the two major parties that had emerged after the civil war of 1922–23: Fianna Fáil and Fine Gael. The political parties were generally centrist and conservative. There was little support among the electorate for radical socialist or nationalist or free market ideologies. The country was strongly democratic, with lively political debate and high voter turnout at elections. The Civil Service was politically impartial and, if conservative in outlook, was reasonably efficient.

Corruption did exist in the political world, but was not a major problem.

Ireland in the 1950s was in many ways an authoritarian and illiberal society. Corporal punishment was widely used in schools and by parents. Extraordinarily large numbers of people were detained in institutions of one kind or another – particularly asylums and mother and baby homes. Probably more people were detained in institutions per head of population in Ireland than in any other European state outside the Soviet Union. It was disturbingly easy to get a person signed into an asylum or an industrial school – much less easy to get them out. Homosexuality was illegal and – while there were exceptions such as the theatre practitioners Hilton Edwards and his partner Micheál Mac Liammóir, who were quite open about their relationship – the majority of gay men and women led secretive lives in fear of the law.

There was censorship of books and newspapers. In 1957 a theatre director, Alan Simpson, was arrested after a condom allegedly appeared on a stage during a performance of the Tennessee Williams play, *The Rose Tattoo*. Girls who got pregnant outside wedlock were regarded as deeply sinful and were often bundled away to England or sent into a mother and baby home so that they would not bring shame on their families. They were often forced to give their children up for adoption.

Women across society in the 1950s were, in many ways, second-class citizens. They were paid less than men and, if married, were barred from many professions, including teaching, nursing and the Civil Service. Contraception was illegal, as was divorce. The careers to which girls could aspire were limited. There was a strong belief across society that a mother's place was in the home with her children. The high level of emigration among young women and teenage girls was sometimes due to their desire to live in societies where they would be better paid and have more rights and opportunities.

However, 1950s Ireland was in many ways a very stable society. There were strong trade unions and many strikes, but – the IRA campaign apart – very little political violence. The crime rate was low, even in the impoverished city areas where, in later times, drug abuse would lead to a huge increase in crime and anti-social behaviour. Murder was rare and so were assaults. People felt safe leaving their doors open in town and country. However, it should be noted that rape and 'domestic violence' did take place, though they may not have been reported, and vandalism was a problem in many areas. Serious crimes against children took place in many institutions. While drugs such as heroin and cocaine were almost non-existent, alcohol abuse was a major problem.

A growing problem during the decade was road safety. Although there were far fewer cars and a million and a half fewer people, the death toll on Irish roads was higher in the 1950s than today. Drink-driving was one factor in this high level of accidents, as well as the poor quality of roads.

The 1950s was a decade in which religion permeated Irish society to an extraordinary extent. In some ways, the country was almost a theocratic state. The Roman Catholic Church ran the majority of schools, as well as many hospitals and a large network of mother and baby homes, industrial schools and other institutions. Politicians were deferential to the Catholic hierarchy, and priests and nuns were held in huge respect by the majority of people. The Church enjoyed a level of respect and adulation in Ireland similar to that enjoyed by the Queen and the Royal Family in 1950s Britain. Children of the time were raised in households in which family prayers were the norm and attended schools where religion was not merely a subject but a central component of the education system. Children in their thousands attended and took part in large-scale religious events such as Corpus Christi processions. For many children and adults, religious faith brought colour into their drab lives and gave them meaning and comfort. For others, however, it brought pain, trauma and rejection.

The power of the Church was immense. When the bishops objected to a welfare bill aimed at providing free medical services for mothers and children, the Mother and Child Scheme, in 1951, many government ministers withdrew support from the health minister and he resigned. A subsequent health bill was drafted in a way that met the concerns of the Church. The 1952 act legalising adoption in Ireland was also drawn up in consultation with the Church. Indeed, throughout the 1950s, the State and the courts gave rulings that helped the Catholic Church to control children. In 1950, the

Supreme Court ruled that in certain circumstances, the written promise that the non-Catholic partner in a 'mixed' marriage was obliged to make – that the children of the marriage would be raised as Catholics – was legally enforceable by Irish law. The Adoption Act stipulated that adoptive parents must be of the same faith as the child they were adopting. While Desmond Doyle was able to retrieve his children from the church-run orphanages to which they had been sent after their mother had left home, the courts and government ministers still made it almost impossible for such children to be freed from these homes.

Ireland at the time was far from the multi-cultural society it has now become. There were few immigrants and virtually everyone was white and Christian. Relations between Roman Catholics and Protestants were reasonably good, but the two communities tended to keep their distance from each other. Catholics were forbidden to enter Protestant churches and Protestants feared that their children might marry Catholics and be lost to the Protestant community. However, although the Constitution recognised the 'special position of the Catholic Church', there was no discrimination against those of minority faiths and the 1950s saw Protestants hold high positions in the government and Civil Service, and a member of the small Jewish community serve two terms as Lord Mayor of Dublin.

During the 1950s, the health and general quality of life for the majority of Irish people improved greatly.

Reforming politicians such as health minister Noël Browne and doctors such as Dorothy Stopford Price waged a successful campaign against TB, which had been one of the worst killer diseases in early twentieth-century Ireland. By 1959, tuberculosis had been largely eradicated from the country.

Antibiotics and other new drugs also helped combat other killers of children such as diphtheria, scarlet fever and polio. Infant and maternal mortality, which had been disturbingly high at the start of the 1950s, was also greatly reduced. Large-scale house-building programmes ensured that many of the children of the era grew up in homes with running water, proper heating and other amenities that improved their health. Rural electrification also contributed to improving the lives of the Irish people. Begun in 1947, the rural electrification scheme was one of the most important programmes of technological modernisation in Irish history. It gave considerable employment and brought large parts of the country into the twentieth century. For a great many Irish people who lived through the 1950s, the coming of electric light to their village or farm was an event that they would never forget. While there were many areas where poverty remained a real problem, the general living standards of Irish people did improve throughout the decade – although at a much slower rate than in the rest of Europe.

Access to education was also something that gradually improved for the children of 1950s Ireland – although free second-level schooling was something that Ireland would not have until the late 1960s. There were major debates throughout the 1950s on what needed to be done to improve educational standards and ensure that children emerged from school equipped for what one commentator described as 'the struggle of life'. The school leaving age remained at 14 throughout the decade, despite many calls to have it raised, and university education remained the preserve of a privileged minority. Each year, however, the numbers staying on in full- or part-time education after primary schooling increased, and more secondary and vocational schools opened. An extensive school building and rebuilding programme also ensured that the majority of the children of the nation were being educated in modern classrooms with proper heating and sanitation by the decade's end.

The 1950s was a dark time in the economic history of the modern Irish nation. Unemployment was high and economic growth slow, while regular balance-of-payments problems meant that there were cutbacks in government expenditure in areas such as improving infrastructure. Protectionist economic policies intended to protect local industries held back development. Trade unions often operated closed shops and other restrictive practices, which made it hard for young people to find employment in certain trades.

The economic boom that began across Western Europe in the early 1950s left Ireland almost untouched. With little prospect of work at home, the youth of Ireland began to emigrate in numbers not seen since the 1880s. In 1957, the emigration rate was almost as high as the birth rate. The census figures for 1956 and 1961 showed a population in decline – despite the large families that were common at the time. By the end of the 1950s, the population had dropped below 3 million. There were many who felt that the country had no real future at all. However, a corner had already been turned. Under the guidance of civil servants such as T.K. Whittaker and political leaders like Sean Lemass, who became Taoiseach in 1959, economic policies began to change. Protectionism was abandoned and Ireland began to open up to foreign investment and to look to a future in Europe's emerging common market. Those in school in the late 1950s would have a better chance of finding work in their own country than their older siblings.

The country was opening up in other ways too. It joined the Council of Europe and was one of the first nations to ratify the European Convention on Human Rights. In 1955, Ireland was admitted to the United Nations. In 1958, Irish soldiers were deployed on UN peace-monitoring duties for the first time. Many of the boys who grew up in 1950s Ireland would serve with the UN in Cyprus and the Congo in the 1960s.

Agriculture was very important in 1950s Ireland. The political ideology of Ireland since independence had favoured the idea of the country as a nation of farmers. Industry was seen by many politicians as somewhat 'un-Irish'. Well into the 1950s, education ministers placed great emphasis on educating young people for a life in agriculture – though few school leavers wanted to work on farms.

Ireland in the 1950s was still, to a great extent, a country of small farms and small towns. Even in Dublin, farms were to be found within a short distance of the city centre, and Dubliners were accustomed to seeing cattle from the farms of the Midlands being driven through the streets to the markets. Many of the farms were run by bachelors. Although families in both rural and urban Ireland tended to be very large, with twelve or more children not uncommon, the country also had one of the lowest marriage rates in the world and one of the highest ages of marriage as well. This low marriage rate was often linked to issues concerning the inheritance of family farms.

Despite the poor economic state of the nation and an often oppressive church, Ireland in the 1950s had a strong cultural life. Up and down the country, amateur drama and musical societies flourished. The Tostál festivals held annually between 1953 and 1957 involved thousands of people, including many children, in productions of plays, music and other cultural activities intended to promote Ireland to tourists and celebrate the nation's rich heritage. The 1950s saw the birth of significant festivals that remain popular to this day, such as the Wexford Opera Festival, the Dublin Theatre festival and the Athlone All-Ireland Drama Festival. The Irish traditional music organisation, Comhaltas Ceoltoiri Éireann, began in

1951. Increasing numbers of schools gave their pupils the opportunity to learn music, art and drama. National children's art competitions and choir and dance festivals for schoolchildren became commonplace.

Cinema thrived during the 1950s, with children, teenagers and adults often going 'to the pictures' a couple of times a week. Television remained a rarity until the end of the 1950s, with a national TV service not beginning until the end of 1961, but radio was popular – especially, for the young, Radio Luxembourg. Rock and roll reached Ireland between 1955 and 1956, and, here as elsewhere, a teenage culture emerged. Across Ireland, skiffle groups were formed, and this led to the start of the showband era, with people flocking to their nearest community hall to dance to the music of bands that formed in towns across Ireland.

In the area of sport, too, large numbers went weekly to watch Gaelic football and hurling, soccer and rugby. In an age in which there were still relatively few cars, people walked and cycled a great deal and thought nothing of travelling 10 miles or more to a dance or a match. In fact, although heavy smoking was the norm for most Irish people over the age of about 15 at that time, it could be argued that many of them were in some respects healthier than the Irish of the 2010s, because they got more exercise. Obesity was not a major health worry in 1950s Ireland.

The children who grew up in Ireland in the 1950s lived in a world in which they could play on the streets with little fear of being knocked down by cars. Health and safety was not a concern, and they were encouraged to go outside to play and explore. There were no smartphones or iPads, no television or computer games. In some ways it was, perhaps, a more innocent society, in which children remained children for longer than nowadays. But there was a darker side to that society. There were children in 1950s Ireland who were, to all intents and purposes, slaves who worked long hours in industrial schools, laundries and reformatories as cheap labour for religious orders and the State. The rosary beads carried by so many of the devout in Dublin in those years of fervent religious practice were often made by young girls in places such as the Goldenbridge orphanage. The laundry for government departments was done by teenage girls and young women in the Magdalene Laundries in places such as Sean McDermott Street.

In remote parts of rural Ireland such as Letterfrack, children endured a regime of brutality in institutions run by religious orders on behalf of the state. Ireland was by no means unique in the 1950s in treating vulnerable children with such cruelty. Many other countries had similar regimes, but the way in which so many Irish children were deprived of their constitutional rights was a shameful episode in the nation's history.

The 1950s is a decade often recalled with nostalgia in countries such as Britain and the United States. There does not appear to be such nostalgia in Ireland – probably because of the memory of poverty, authoritarianism and a sense that the country had lost its way during those difficult times. Not everything about 1950s Ireland was bad or unhappy, however. This book tells the story of childhood in that decade – home life, schooling, entertainment, religion and other aspects of life – in an era so very different from the society in which today's Irish children, the grandchildren of the children of the 1950s, are growing up.

Acknowledgements

I wish to express my deep gratitude to all those people who shared their memories of being a child in 1950s Ireland with me.

I also wish to thank the staffs of the National Library of Ireland, Dublin City Libraries, Westmeath County Library, the Mullingar Cathedral Archives, *The Cork Examiner* and Mr Gearoid O'Brien for their help in providing photographs and other material. I also want to thank Sgt Roger Nicholson, Mullingar Garda Station, for allowing me to study a school's attendance records book for Co. Westmeath.

Thanks to Joan Greene and Joe Gallagher at Lir Business Centre, Mullingar, for their help typing up the manuscript.

Thanks also to Alex Waite, Ronan Colgan, Jessicca Gofton and Caitlin Kirkman at The History Press.

Timeline of the 1950s in Ireland

1950

Dogma of the Assumption of the Virgin Mary proclaimed by Pope Pius XII on 1 November. Ceremonies are held across Ireland to mark the event.

A Supreme Court ruling in what is known as the Tilson Case states that, in certain circumstances, the promise made by the non-Catholic partner in a marriage to have the children of the marriage raised in the Roman Catholic faith may be legally binding.

Although adoption is not legal in Ireland, a significant number of babies and toddlers are given to American couples for adoption in 1950 and in 1951. Ireland gains a reputation in the USA as a place where couples wishing to adopt may find babies. The babies come from mother and baby homes and other institutions.

1951

Mother and Child Scheme put forward by health minister Noël Browne. The scheme proposes free healthcare for all new mothers and for all children under 16. The Scheme is opposed by the Roman Catholic Church, the Irish Medical Organisation and some of Dr Browne's colleagues. He resigns from government and the coalition government collapses.

1952

Adoption Act legalises adoption in Ireland. Children aged between six months and 7 years may be adopted if they are orphans or illegitimate. Adoptive parents must be of the same religion as the child's mother. Overseas adoption allowed only if the child is illegitimate.

Youth organisation Macra na Tuaithe (now Foróige) set up 'to allow young people to involve themselves consciously and actively in their development and in the development of society.'

1953

The Health Act introduces free healthcare for babies up to six weeks old and mothers.

The first An Tostál (pageant) cultural festival is held. Children and teenagers play a major role in many of the events. The Tostál will take place again in 1954, 1955 and 1956.

1954

Infant mortality drops to the lowest rate ever recorded in Ireland.

Marian Year dedicated to honouring the Virgin Mary. Ceremonies take place across Ireland, many involving children and teenagers.

A general election takes place. Fianna Fáil lose power to a coalition government headed by Fine Gael. John Costello returns as Taoiseach.

1955

Ireland joins the United Nations.

The Supreme Court rules that the children of Dublin father Desmond Doyle should be returned to him. The children had been placed in orphanages and industrial schools after their mother left the family and moved to England. The Children Act of 1941 decreed that a deserted father could not have custody of his children and care of them unless the mother gave her written consent. The ruling in the Doyle case led to the Act being amended.

A German newspaper reports that around 1,000 children have been removed from Ireland over the last three years for adoption.

Rock and roll reaches Ireland. Concerns are raised about violent comics from America.

1956

Polio outbreak in Cork affects many children. Special day of prayer and blessing held for children in July.

Census shows a fall in the population. Unemployment and emigration increase.

Senator Owen Sheehy-Skeffington introduces a bill in the Senate seeking the abolition of corporal punishment in schools for girls.

The Irish Society for the Prevention of Cruelty to Children comes into existence, replacing the British-run National Society for the Prevention of Cruelty to Children.

Crumlin Children's Hospital opens in Dublin.

The IRA begins a military campaign against Northern Ireland. Known as the Border Campaign, it will last until 1962. The Catholic bishops warn young people not to get involved with the IRA or other illegal societies.

Children and teenagers are among a number of Hungarian refugees brought to Ireland after the Soviet invasion of Hungary.

Concerns about the illegal adoption of children are raised in the Dáil by Deputy Maureen O'Carroll.

1957

Emigration accelerates as the economy remains in a poor state. Net emigration almost equals the birth rate. Children and teenagers are among those leaving the country.

The Fethard-on-Sea boycott begins. A Protestant woman living in the Co. Wexford village of Fethard moves back to Belfast, bringing her children with her so that they will not be brought up as Catholics. Believing that local Protestants helped her to leave, Roman Catholics begin a boycott of Protestant shops and businesses. The boycott is defended by Catholic bishops but is condemned by Taoiseach Eamon De Valera and other Catholics. One Catholic bishop claims that an attempt is being made to 'steal' Catholic children from their faith.

Two IRA volunteers, Sean South and Fergal O'Hanlon, are killed during an attack on a police station in Northern Ireland. Their funerals, in Limerick and Co. Monaghan, are attended by thousands of people, including many children and teenagers.

The third general election in six years leads to the return to power of Fianna Fáil.

The 1941 Children Act is amended to allow children placed in care because a parent has deserted the home to be returned to the remaining parent. However, it remains almost impossible for parents to retrieve their children.

The Soviet Sputnik space probe is seen over Ireland, emitting a beeping signal heard by radio operators around the world.

1958

The ban on married women working as teachers is lifted.

Dr T.K. Whittaker becomes secretary of the Department of Finance. The Irish government begins to move towards a new economic policy of ending protectionism and encouraging industrialisation and multi-national investment in Ireland.

Thousands of Irish children and teenagers take part in an international pilgrimage to Lourdes to mark the centenary of the Marian vision there.

The Dublin-born Manchester United player Liam 'Billy' Whelan is killed in the Munich air disaster. Pupils from his old school in Dublin are among the thousands who line the streets to pay tribute as the funeral cortège passes through the city.

The Salk polio vaccine is administered in Ireland for the first time following a polio outbreak in the Midlands.

More than ninety new schools are opened during the academic year 1958–59.

1959
....

Sean Lemass becomes Taoiseach. The government programme of modernising and opening up the Irish economy accelerates.

Women are recruited into the Gardaí for the first time.

Ulster Television begins broadcasting from Belfast. With TV signals from the UK now being picked up along the east coast of Ireland and the Border region, the number of televisions in Ireland begins to increase.

1

Infancy

For many children in Ireland in the 1950s, life began in the home. While increasing numbers of babies were born in hospital, home births were still very common. Mothers gave birth with the assistance of district nurses or midwives. In some areas, where electric light did not yet exist, babies entered the world with tilly lamps or even candles providing light. Fathers were rarely present at the births of their children, because it was considered unseemly for them to be there. They waited in another room of the house, or, if the birth was in hospital, at home.

Baptisms were performed within days of the birth. This was due to a doctrine then promulgated by the Roman Catholic Church that held that if a baby died unbaptised, it could not enter heaven but was instead assigned eternally to a place called limbo. While life expectancy and medical care had greatly improved in twentieth-century

Ireland, the country still had, at the start of the 1950s, the highest infant mortality rate in Western Europe, so it was considered essential that babies be baptised as soon as possible after birth.

The baby was brought to church by the father and godparents. While the baptism took place, the mother sat at the back of the church or outside. She could not take part in a sacrament such as baptism until she had been put through a purification ceremony known as 'churching', which made her spiritually clean again in the eyes of the Church. After baptism, the baby was well wrapped up and brought home. Visitors and family members placed holy medals or silver coins on the baby's cot or pram to bring good luck to the baby. The medals were seen as providing spiritual protection, while the silver coins were believed to ensure that as an adult the baby would escape poverty and live to a ripe old age. The coin would also bring good luck to the person who placed it on the cot.

The prams of the era were generally large and the baby was high off the ground – unlike the strollers of modern times. In fine weather, the pram would be wheeled outside so that the baby could get fresh air and sunshine. While men accompanied their wives and infants on walks, it was rare for a father to be seen wheeling the pram on his own.

Breastfeeding was in decline in 1950s Ireland and formula feeding, from manufacturers such as Cow and Gate, was becoming the fashion. The feeding bottles used included upright Pyrex or boat-shaped ones, with one or two rubber teats. In rural areas, newborns were often given milk from a calving cow to build up their immune system. This milk was known as 'bisnings'. As the infant moved on to solid foods, they would often be placed in a high chair at meal times. The chair would have a bar inserted between two holes across the front to secure the child.

Prams were sometimes converted into toddler go-karts, and old tea chests used as play-pens. One woman recalled how her father, who was a tailor, used to 'pad the top rim of the tea chests with scraps of material and do the same with the inside, for the comfort and safety of the little ones'.

Families in 1950s Ireland were often very large. Four or five children in a family would be the norm – six to eight children was quite common and nine or more not a rarity. Some parents raised families of twelve or even fourteen. Older children helped in the rearing of the younger ones, wheeling the pram, bathing, dressing and feeding their siblings. Many large families were raised in two-bedroom houses and it was normal practice for children to share beds. Two or three children could be fitted into one bed and there could be two or even three beds in one room. Small cottages, which might now be lived in by one person, could have had twelve or more occupants.

Advertisements in the papers for smart new outfits for 'kiddies' appeared daily in the national and local press. In 1958, for example, *The Cork Examiner* advertised Roches Store's offers of 'Kiddies' jumpers at 16/3s and slacks at

19/3/9*d*', but not all parents could afford to buy new clothes. There were high levels of poverty in Ireland at the time, with an economy that, until the last years of the decade, was actually contracting. So in many households, clothes were made rather than bought, and handed down from child to child. The clothes were patched up when tears appeared. Likewise, shoes were repaired, not replaced. Many houses had a last for putting patches on soles and tips on heels, and when new soles were needed the shoes were brought to the cobblers.

Clothes were often worn for several days in a row as washing machines and spin dryers were not in existence. Clothes were serviceable rather than fashionable. The family laundry was usually done on one day of the week, often a Monday, and this involved manual scrubbing. Before the arrival of electricity, water was boiled up on a range and a large tub used for the wash. The whole process of scrubbing clothes with a brush and drying them usually took the entire day. Boys usually wore short trousers and a shirt with braces. Girls wore pinafore dresses or smocks, and cardigans and vests, with socks.

In wet weather, children often wore wellingtons, which were polished using Vaseline. A big excitement for many children was the arrival of parcels of new clothes from relatives in Britain or America. What were known as 'American parcels' would often contain white suits and bright check sports coats, or brightly coloured dresses, that would dazzle the eye.

Food

The children of the 1950s usually had a plain, healthy diet. In rural districts, and even in urban areas, families often grew their own food. Many households were all but completely self-sufficient, with only tea and sugar being bought. Cabbage, lettuce, carrots and turnips were grown; bread was baked, and cheese and butter were made at home as well. Farm families usually had pigs, turkeys, ducks and hens. Before preparing meals, parents and children would go outside and collect the food growing in their garden.

Where food was bought rather than home-produced, the shopping was done on a daily basis as there were no freezers until late in the decade, and not many fridges either. The average daily food shop took up to an hour, with one shopping bag being used for many years. Children ate the same meals as their parents, just in smaller portions. Bread and butter, porridge, bacon and cabbage, chicken, stews and mushy peas were the normal fare. The bread was usually home-made. Potatoes were grated raw to make 'boxty' – a traditional potato pancake – or boiled and mashed with butter, salt, pepper and spring onions to make concannon. In summer, mushrooms were taken home, peeled, placed on a hot coal and served with a pinch of salt.

For Roman Catholics, Friday was a no-meat day so fish was consumed instead, with ling a popular choice of fish. Fish and chips was a popular dish in urban areas.

Eggs were also consumed, although not so much in rural areas where the eggs were brought to market to be sold rather than eaten at home. On farms, the cock chickens were reared for the table while the hens were kept for laying. Soups were usually made up from a variety of vegetables. Barley, lentils and peas were mixed into a broth and boiled up from bones acquired from butchers; in parts of Dublin this concoction was known as 'soup confetti'. Ketchup was also home-made and bottled for storage.

Dessert was usually a luxury reserved for Sundays or special occasions such as birthdays or Christmas. Popular desserts included custard and jelly, ice cream, or stewed apple tart. Favourite foods for children included 'cally' or 'champ' – a dish of new potatoes with a well of butter and scallions (spring onions) and 'goody' – bread baked in hot milk with sugar or raisins. There was also what was known as 'bang bang', which was warm bread fresh from the bakery cut up into thick wedges and smeared with butter and jam, washed down with milk.

Fruit was considered something of a luxury in many households. As one man recalled, 'There was no such thing as buying fruit and putting it into a fruit bowl to look at it!' Apples, plums, bananas and blackberries and raspberries were favourite fruits, and the apples, blackberries and raspberries were often gathered by children during holiday times or on their way to and from school. These seasonal fruits were preserved to make jams.

Popular sweets included toffees, penny bars, gob-stoppers and sticks of rock. Crisps were also popular – particularly after the invention of the Tayto crisp in 1954. Cleeves Slab Toffee, 4½p for a slab, 'equalled four days of blissful slobbering'. For many children, their weekly pocket money of 6p could buy a bar of Cadbury's Fruit and Nut, or thirty-six honeybee toffees or eighteen Nancy balls (aniseed), six 'fix' bags, six liquorice strings and a tar-black sweet called 'cough no more' described by the writer Deirdre Purcell as 'not for the faint-hearted'. A favourite sweet or dessert in Dublin was what was known as gur cake. This was made from stale bread soaked in black tea, with currants, raisins and sugar topped with pastry.

Children drank a lot of milk, as well as Bovril, cocoa and tea. Lemonade was often home-made, but soft drinks like MiWadi, which could be bought in local shops, were also popular. For some children, a once-a-week treat was a cup of Nescafé spooned from a tiny round tin and made with hot milk. Buttermilk was given to children, particularly in country areas. It was believed to be very good for children's health, and boys were told it would put hair on their chests. There was a tradition on Good Friday in country areas of gathering eggs that had just been laid. These eggs were known as *clúdoe* and were eaten on Easter Sunday.

Illness

To deal with childhood ailments, a variety of medicines were available to parents. Sick children were dosed with cod liver oil, syrup of figs, milk of magnesia, gripe water, Epsom salts, castor oil and petroleum jelly. Red flannel was used to treat colds and chest infections. Lucozade was regarded as a medicine at that time, and was given to children suffering from 'flu. The age of antibiotics had begun, so 1950s children were safe from the epidemics of diphtheria and scarlet fever that had claimed so many young lives in earlier times. Tuberculosis, however, remained a threat well into the 1950s in many parts of the country, although the disease diminished as new vaccines and better housing were introduced.

Polio was another serious health scourge, which afflicted children and teens as well as adults. There was a major epidemic in the Cork region in 1956, which led to the closure of schools, the postponement of sporting events and the cancellation of a planned circus visit to the city. Cork families working in England postponed planned holiday visits home. Children were warned to stay away from crowds and refrain from excessive exercise. Parents were encouraged to have their children in bed before nightfall. When the Cork/Kildare All-Ireland Football semi-final was not cancelled, a Dublin mother wrote to the papers condemning the GAA and the Minister for Health for not stopping the match. She wrote, 'it will be us mothers who will have the anxiety and sorrow if our children are struck down.' Parents were requested not to bring children under 14 to the match. Seventy-one of the ninety cases notified in Cork city were children under 10, and one child died.

Those children who contracted polio and survived went through a miserable time, often spending the whole day in a large machine known as an iron lung, which helped them to breathe. The experience was described by one patient as 'similar to lying in a coffin with one's head sticking out'. One woman recalled how she 'spent four years of my childhood in hospital after being diagnosed with polio aged 17 months. Due to the progressive treatment of the day, thankfully I recovered well in my early teens.' One of the most poignant images of the era was of small children on crutches with their legs encased in callipers.

Towards the end of the 1950s, a new polio vaccine developed in America was introduced into Ireland and the terror of polio faded away, although parents sometimes had to be persuaded to get their children vaccinated.

In 1955, there was a serious outbreak of gastroenteritis, which led to more than twenty children being hospitalised. The outbreak was linked to the impoverished conditions in which many Dublin children lived. Ringworm was another unpleasant infection that many children contracted. Those suffering from this illness spent many weeks in hospital and had to have their hair shaved.

Mumps, measles, rubella and chickenpox were the most common infectious illnesses affecting children in the 1950s. There was no MMR vaccine and it was considered that these illnesses were something children were almost guaranteed to get and a part of childhood. When a child got measles or mumps, the other children in the household would sometimes be put in the same bed as the sick one so that they could catch the disease and, as it were, get it out of the way. One man remembered how he was 'put in with' his sisters when they came down with measles, 'so we would all get it at the same time'. In the 1950s there was an average of 8,500 cases of measles in Ireland per year.

Housing

During the 1950s, the houses in which many children grew up were devoid of central heating or running water. Open fires provided warmth in the kitchen or sitting room area. In some rooms, what the writer Alice Taylor described as 'evil smelling' oil heaters were used. In winter months the windows were frosted up, with the frost often on the inside of the window. Rather than the duvets of today, children slept under layers of heavy blankets. One man whose father was a soldier remembered how his father's army greatcoat provided considerable warmth on cold winter nights. Chilblains were a frequent childhood affliction due to cold houses, with many suffering with swollen chilblained fingers and toes, which were very painful. Many houses had no bathrooms or indoor toilets. Like their parents, children trooped outside to a loo in the backyard.

Saturday night was traditionally bath night in many households as the family prepared for church the following day. The water, which sometimes came from a pump or well or was collected from a rain barrel, would be boiled up in a tin bath and placed before the fire. Children bathed singly or together, removing, as writer Alice Taylor described it, 'the mud, grass, earth, hay, dust and chaff that perfumed our daily lives'. After the bath, the lice comb was used, and girls had their hair tied up in rags and pipe cleaners to tease their curls – which made for an uncomfortable night's sleep. 'Sunday best' clothes were worn to church. Boys usually had short hair, with the hair being cut at home or at the barber's, where they sat on a plank that went across the arms of the barber's chair.

For many children in the 1950s in rural parts of Ireland, electric light was unknown. At home they played and did their homework by candlelight or oil lamps, and carried candles up to their bedrooms. In some towns, gas lighting continued well into the 1950s. Alice Taylor recalled how, in her Cork home, 'we experienced the tilly lamp as a big breakthrough into a world of light in about 1950'. The tilly lamp was fed on oil and gave a much stronger light. Tilly heaters also came into use.

The rural electrification scheme, which began in 1947, gradually extended electric light across the country and for many children, one of the most memorable events of their childhood was the coming of electricity to their village or farm. They watched the gradual advance of electricity poles towards their house, with one boy remembering coming home from school to find the electricity switched on. In villages up and down the country, young and old would gather for a special ceremony where the lights would be switched on by local dignitaries. Alice Taylor wrote about how electric light 'made the journey upstairs to bed much less frightening. It was now no longer necessary to check under beds for lurking spooks or to peer through shadowy doorways for silent figures waiting to pounce.'

It was a thrill for many children to be able to flick a switch and see the room filled with light, and to be able to read in bed or play board games without straining their eyes. A cartoon in the magazine *Dublin Opinion* showed parents watching the installation of electricity and saying 'how great it was that their children would now be able to study all night for the Civil Service.'

A major improvement in the lives of children in urban areas was the move to new council houses. In cities and towns there was a large-scale public housebuilding programme, which brought thousands of families out of slum housing and into new suburbs and estates (the Finglas area of Dublin for example). These new houses were usually two or three bedroom with small gardens that were often used to grow food as well as flowers. The houses had electricity and fireplaces, some also had central heating and indoor toilets. Although small and cramped by modern standards, these council houses were a massive improvement on the housing left behind.

As recalled by many who grew up in these new city suburbs or the new estates in country towns, the streets 'rang with the cries of van men selling vegetables, bread, meat and fish'. Pig swill was collected in barrels balanced on a cart by a person known as the 'slops man'. Coal was delivered to the back garden shed, and rag-and-bone men collected unwanted furniture and other items. The smells of the era included manure from the animals brought along the streets to market, the acrid smell of coal dust, and the 'alcoholicy scent from breweries and distilleries'.

Children in the 1950s usually had their mother at home during the day. Society of the day expected women to stay at home and care for their children. Articles were published in women's magazines stating that it was vital for the welfare and good development of the child that the mother should be at home, and juvenile delinquency was blamed by many on absentee mothers. Few mothers worked outside the home, in part because of the marriage ban that forced women in many public service jobs such as teaching and the civil service to resign when they married.

However, a lot of children did have mothers who, despite raising big families, were also working in family businesses such as shops and farms. One Athlone woman recalled:

My mother was always pregnant (ten children in fifteen years). Our house was full of children – so was every house in our street. My own mother was a well educated, well-read woman who helped in our family business.

She also recalled mothers of friends who ran shops, hairdressing salons and even a dental practice.

A few women who were retired teachers set up preschools where children aged 3 to 5 were taught to read, write and count. Crèches were almost non-existent. The large families of the time meant that, even before they started school, children learned to socialise, playing with their neighbours' children, with parents looking out for each of the children in the neighbourhood, not just their own. While it was generally mothers who cared for the children, there were many cases where widowed fathers brought up large families.

2

Primary School

In the mid 1950s, there were about 476,000 children enrolled in some 5,000 primary schools across Ireland. These schools educated children between the ages of 4 and 14. For the vast majority of the children of 1950s Ireland, the primary or national school would be the only formal education they would receive. Most of the schools were run by the Roman Catholic Church, the Church of Ireland or other Protestant denominations. Local parish priests or ministers were the school managers, and the local bishop the school patron. For infants starting off in convent schools, the nuns could be terrifying figures in their old-fashioned black habits and veils.

In urban areas, the teachers in the Roman Catholic schools often belonged to religious orders – priests, nuns or brothers. In country areas, teachers were usually laypeople. Married women were banned from teaching until 1958. According to the State, the purpose of the primary school was:

> to assist and supplement the work of parents in the rearing of their children. Their first duty is to train their children in the fear and love of God. That duty becomes the first purpose of the primary school. It is fulfilled by the school through the religious and moral training of the child, through the teaching of good habits and through the instruction in the duties of citizenship and the pupil's obligations to his parents and community.

Starting school, 'the great adventure' as one man remembered it, generally began on or around a child's fourth birthday. The school year started on 1 July, and children normally moved up a class or entered or finished their schooling at the end of June. The child beginning school would start off in what was variously referred to as 'baby infants' or 'low babies'. In low babies and high babies (or senior infants), children were introduced to reading, writing and counting. In some schools, a sandpit was provided in which children were shown how to draw letters and numbers in the sand. A modelling clay known in Irish as 'marla' was used, too. Slates were given to the pupils with pieces of chalk and crayons. One woman recalls how:

Mrs Raleigh used to go round the classroom saying, 'This is Kate the cat speaking.' This was a story in an English reader which we all had for years, and so she had it off by heart, as we all did eventually.

One of the major aims of the educational authorities after Irish Independence was achieved in 1922 was to revive the Irish language and make the country at least bilingual. To this end, in many primary schools, the majority of subjects were taught in Irish. So, for the vast majority of the children, school was where they first heard and learned what was officially held to be the first national language.

One man whose schooling began in the 1950s remembered that the first words of Irish he was taught were *madra* (dog) and *cát* (cat)! One very important phrase was *an bhfuil cead agam dul amach go dti an leithreas?* ('May I go out to the toilet?') As the children progressed through school, they acquired a *mala* (bag). The first official Gaelscoil (Irish school) opened in Dublin in 1952.

For children with disabilities, a number of schools existed – but only in the Dublin area, where there were two schools for blind children and two for deaf. By the end of the decade, however, around 2,600 children with a variety of disabilities were being educated in fourteen institutions around the country, nearly all run by religious orders.

The school buildings to which the children went varied much in quality. In 1952, the Minister for

Education admitted that 10 per cent of schools were 'derelict'. A quarter of the primary school buildings were 100 or more years old. An editorial in the *Irish Independent* in 1956 deplored the fact that Ireland's countryside was 'dotted with dilapidated buildings, which anybody with any national pride would be ashamed to admit to a tourist are schools'. Many children of the era sat in draughty, ill-lit rooms, with little heating and poor sanitation. There were schools in which draughts blew through holes in the windows and rats scurried around the classroom.

However, as the decade progressed the situation improved, with an average of forty-five new primary school buildings being erected annually – increasing to more than 100 a year by 1959. Many children experienced a huge improvement in their environment as they moved into bright, clean and warm new classrooms in buildings with indoor toilets. In 1956, for example, a new school was opened in Kingscourt, Co. Cavan, by the Roman Catholic Bishop of Meath, Dr John Kyne, in which the 246 students had classrooms built on 'most modern lines, with mahogany desks'.

The new St Patrick's School in Bray, run by the De La Salle Order and opened by Archbishop John McQuaid of Dublin in 1955, provided pupils and their teachers with 'six large classrooms, a teachers' staff room and amenities'. In 1958, a new school for more than 800 children, with more than thirty rooms and play areas outside, was opened in Athy, Co. Kildare.

Many of these schools were part funded by parents and other parishioners – for example £30,000 was raised for the new Carmelite school in Moate, Co. Westmeath. In Limerick, a group of children aged between 5 and 12 put on a concert to help raise funds for an extension to a convent school in the city. They put on a special performance at the concert for the nuns in the school and were rewarded with tea and cakes by the appreciative sisters.

Many 1950s children had good memories of their new school buildings. One Christian Brothers primary was described by a past pupil as: 'The state of the art in architectural design and accommodation, with each classroom taking advantage of ample daylight, with waist-high windows, to the roof on one wall.'

A past pupil in a rural school recalled:

Our surprise and delight on entering our new school – everything brand spanking new. The new two-seater desks with ink wells with sliding covers that worked! There were new wall maps and cloakrooms, flush toilets with wash hand basins and hot and cold running water.

For children, the school day usually began at 9 a.m. The majority of children walked to school, and in rural areas the walk could be 2 or 3 miles or longer. In 1956, a letter from a 'Galway girl' in the *Sunday Independent* described the plight of her siblings aged 12, 11 and 9, who had to leave home at 8.15 a.m. to walk 2 miles to school 'carrying a ridiculous amount of books on their backs. Whenever they are late, they are caned or kept back in school for an extra hour. They have only a few sandwiches to eat between 8.00 a.m. and 4.00/5.00 p.m.' A wealthy Irish-American businessman read this letter and bought bicycles for the three children.

Even in the towns few people owned cars until late in the 1950s, and even bicycles were scarce, although one Westmeath man remembers being brought to school on his mother's bicycle carrier when he was an infant. In one Roscommon school, on wet days pupils were lucky enough to get a lift in a teacher's car. A Co. Mayo teacher acted as the 'school transport system'. In the summertime, country children often walked barefoot. They met up with neighbouring children along the way, and the older ones looked after the younger ones.

In many schools, before the arrival of electricity, schoolrooms were heated by open fires. The pupils brought sods of turf or bundles of sticks (*cipíní*) to school with them. Families took it in turn to supply fuel for the school. In some schools, turf was delivered by horse and cart and the children helped to load the turf into the schoolhouse shed. On arrival, older pupils had the job of lighting the fires or ranges in the classrooms. As one woman recalled:

Children were so resourceful and responsible – I was lighting the Stanley range in our schoolroom at the age of 8, using rolled-up paper, *cipíní* and paraffin oil.

The heaters in the schools could be a real problem. In one Westmeath school, an oil heater used to belch forth such quantities of smoke that the pupils (much to their delight) often had to evacuate the classroom for a time. The fires were lit before school started, but it sometimes took until the middle of the day for the smouldering turf or wood to get going properly. Many a child, arriving in school on a wet or cold morning, spent much of the day sitting in damp clothes, shivering. Some teachers organised vigorous PE sessions to warm up their pupils.

Not surprisingly, many parents kept infants away from school during the depths of winter. Even when the fires were blazing or the heaters working, there could still be problems. One man recalled that his teacher was in the habit of standing in front of the fireplace, blocking off the heat from the pupils! When electricity reached rural schools, the quality of life for children and teachers improved immeasurably. Central heating was installed and children recall gathering around the heaters on winter mornings – they could now dry their wet coats properly.

School days started with prayers, often in Irish. The educational authorities, as well as the churches, felt that spirituality should permeate the classroom. After the morning prayer, the roll was called with each pupil calling out '*anseo*' ('here') when his or her name was read out. The day's work then began.

Children generally sat two together on benches with a large wooden desk in front of them. An important component of the desk was the inkwell. The ink was made up from a powder, sometimes by the pupils themselves, and the inkwells had a sliding brass cover. One of the early lessons for pupils was how to write using ink without creating blots and spills. If the child leaned on the nib too hard, the ink would flow straight onto the exercise book, resulting in ink blotches that no amount of rubbing would erase. The *peann agus dúch* (pen and ink) was disliked by many pupils, but biros were not allowed by the Department of Education until the mid 1960s.

Pencils were also used, and children learned to write using lined exercise books. One man recalled, 'We wrote with long-handled pens like old scribes.' Slates were also used, with red and blue lines as a writing guide, and sums done on the black side of the slate. There was much emphasis on teaching children to write clearly and properly – both printing and joined-up handwriting. The teacher would stand at the blackboard, chalk in hand, to display how to form the various letters correctly. The pupils would copy out lines such as 'Hills far away are green', 'All that glitters is not gold' and 'Eaten bread is not forgotten'.

For left-handed children, learning to write could be a real problem, for in the 1950s, there was a general belief that left-handedness was some kind of aberration that should be discouraged at all costs. Many left-handed adults recall being hit with a ruler to be forced to use their right hand. There were enlightened teachers who allowed the use of the left hand when it was obvious to them that the child could not write properly with the right, but they were very much the exception.

In most classrooms, there were maps of Ireland and the world on the walls. The blackboard – *clár dubh* in Irish – usually stood on an often rickety easel beside or behind the teacher's desk. This was the era of 'chalk and talk', with the teacher writing up sums and spellings and facts to be learned, which the children copied in their books. Children were also brought up to work out sums or spellings on the board – a matter of dread for those who did not know the right answers or who were slow to understand what was being taught.

Special needs assistants did not exist in the schools of the 1950s, and while provisions were made for the schooling of deaf and blind children, there was almost no knowledge of dyslexia, autism or other learning difficulties. The classroom could be a very difficult place indeed for such children. Official reports criticised the way in which the education system treated 'backward' pupils. In one school, a boy with what would now be called special needs was put standing on a desk and mocked by his teacher for not knowing the right answer to a question.

While most children, particularly in the towns and cities, were educated in schools with five, six or more classrooms, a lot of rural children went to one- or two-room schools where wooden partitions divided a room in two, with one or two classes being taught on either side of the partition. Alice Taylor has written about how, in her primary school, if she got bored with what her own teacher was teaching, she would listen to what was being taught to the other class – an 'open plan education'. One former pupil at a Midlands school credited her ability to follow two different conversations at the same time, or read two books or papers simultaneously, to her classroom days listening to two different teachers at the same time!

There were still – though the number was dwindling – a significant number of one-teacher schools, where the teacher single-handedly taught a schoolroom of pupils ranging in age from 4 to 14. In such schools, pupils in one year would be given written work to do, while the teacher taught other pupils, and the older pupils helped to teach the younger ones. In two-teacher schools, one room was generally for infant and junior classes, while senior pupils were in the other room, or boys were in one class and girls in another. Even in two-, three- or four-teacher schools, the number of pupils in each class was often very large. It was not unusual to have forty, fifty or even more children in one class. There were even schools with up to ninety children in a class, although the education authorities were trying to ensure that no class contained more than forty children. As late as 1962, there were still over 1,100 one- or two-teacher schools in the country.

Perhaps because teachers had to cope with so many pupils, discipline in the 1950s Irish school was usually very strict and sometimes savage. In every classroom there was what was called a *bathá* (stick or cane), or a 'lath' or 'leather'. One Westmeath man still vividly remembers fifty years on, 'the sting of the blue lath' that, in his school, was kept at the back of the stove and used for breaches of discipline. The Dublin-born writer Desmond Ellis describes the leather as 'an instrument of torture'.

In the Christian Brothers schools, 'the leather' was used, often with great ferocity and enthusiasm. Boys were sometimes given six blows on each hand and some teachers used rulers – hitting children over the knuckles, as well as on the palms, or on the backs of their legs. Canes made from bamboo or hazel were also used. Some children even had to provide the sticks used for corporal punishment: 'You cut it, brought it back and quite often you were the first to get beat with it.'

Children were also, in some schools, hit with blackboard dusters, boxed on the ears, slapped on the face or pulled around by the hair. A girl from Co. Kerry who was taught by nuns recalled that pupils were 'abused right, left and centre, really and truly. Slaps and all the rest of it and the belt.'

One man remembered his experience of a Christian Brothers school in the Midlands:

The men in black carried custom-made leather weapons in the pockets of their long cassocks. The leather was the common denominator of things educational. A fellow clanged a bell in the morning that was the signal to line up in the yard to march into school in two lines. We line up again to march out to the jacks (toilets) at break time. They were the proud possessors of a multi-urinal where about ten could perform at the same time. You had to go whether you needed to or not. When the bell rang to signal break was over, we lined up all over again and clogged our way back to class two by two to the call of '*Clé/Deas Clé/Deas*' (left/right), teaching a mixture of learning, marching, Gaelic, Chastisement and Religion.

While most teachers used corporal punishment for offences such as giving cheek, fighting in the playground or not having homework done, there were those who believed that knowledge had to be beaten into children. In the Senate, Owen Sheehy-Skeffington, who campaigned throughout his political career for an end to corporal punishment, detailed cases where children had been subjected to merciless beatings by teachers who seemed to lose all self-control. Then education minister Richard Mulcahy accused Sheehy-Skeffington of being anti-Irish and of wanting to bring in alien values to the country. But, while complaints were sometimes made and children were removed from certain schools by parents, the general feeling appears to have been that, if a child was beaten, they had done something to deserve it. The child was even sometimes beaten again by a parent for having done something wrong at school. As one man remembered, 'You kept quiet about the punishment you had received or you got punished again.' The Ireland of the 1950s was an authoritarian and often harsh society in which Gardaí, clergy and teachers were revered and respected. At school, 'the teacher always ruled'. There was often little respect for children at that time.

The main subjects taught in primary school were Irish, English, Arithmetic, Geography, History and Religion. The main focus was on what was referred to as 'the 4 Rs' – reading, writing, 'rithmetic and religion. The main way in which the 4 Rs were taught usually involved a fifth 'R' – rote learning.

Irish

Irish was considered the most important subject in many schools, and there were many where it was the language of instruction for all subjects except English and Religious Education – the Roman Catholic Church insisted that children must be taught religion in their mother tongue. In many cases children were completely lost because they could not understand anything they were being taught. Others managed to learn well enough. Many adults today educated in the 1950s can still do mental arithmetic in Irish!

The teaching of Irish put much emphasis on grammar rules and less on spoken Irish. The pupils learned the tenses, *Aimsir Chaite*, *Aimsir Ghnathcháite* and *Aimsir Fhaistineach* (past, present, future); grammar and vocabulary was learned off by heart and chanted in rote: 'We knew our *tuaisals* and *aimsirs* (verb tenses) inside out. We learned "*liom, leat, leis, lei, linn, libh, leo*" (with me, with you, with him, with her, with us, with them, with those).'

Compositions in Irish were usually on topics such as '*Lá cois fharraige*' ('A day at the seaside'). The trick was to extend the essay with detailed descriptions of what one ate and drank for breakfast, and to name everyone you met on the way to school, so you could limit the amount of vocabulary you used in the essay and avoided the more difficult, harder words and sentence constructions. An example might be:

D'eirigh me ar a h'ocht a clog. D'itheann me mo bricfeasta. Itheann me arán, agus im agus porridge agus d'ol me bainne. Chuaigh me go dtí an scoil. Bhi Maire, Aine agus Sean agus Norinn agus Seamus ag dul do dtí an scoil freisin, Bhi an aimsir go h'aileann.
[I got up at eight o'clock, I ate breakfast. I ate bread and butter and porridge and drank milk. I went to school. Maire, Sean and Noreen and Seamus were going to school as well. The weather was beautiful.]

In learning Irish then, children also had to master a new script, since Irish then had its own script known as *seimhiú* (the Latin/Roman script now used was adopted in the 1960s). Poems were learned off by heart and, in some schools, children were even encouraged to compose poetry. The poets studied by the children included Patrick Pearse.

Geography

Geography class focused on learning the names of Irish counties, rivers, mountains and towns. Pupils learned to chant the 'Three Sisters' (the rivers Barrow, Nore and Suir), the names of the four provinces, the county towns, and the products of each town. For example:

An Gallimh (Galway): fisheries, woollens, marble, millinery, agricultural implements, University College
Béal Átha Na Sluaighe (Ballinasloe): boots and shoes, cattle, horse and sheep fairs
An Tuaim (Tuam): sugar factory
Ath Luáin (Athlone): woollens, cotton and linen

The names of foreign countries and their capital cities and chief industries were also learned off by heart. The geography books studied included *Tir-Eolas na Helropa* (Knowledge of the Land of Europe) and *Tir-Eolas na hÉireann* (Knowledge of the Land of Ireland).

History

History focused mostly on Ireland. While British children were learning about kings and queens of England, Irish children were learning about battles and rebellions during Ireland's '800-year struggle for freedom' from English rule. The focus of history was on Ireland's Catholic and Gaelic heritage and her 'Golden Age of Christianity', which provided artworks such as the Book of Kells.

In place of kings and queens, Irish children were taught to revere men (women didn't really feature) such as Owen Roe O'Neill, Wolfe Tone, Daniel O'Connell and Patrick Pearse (whose poems formed part of both the Irish and English curriculum). The pupils also learned about the The Great Famine (*An Gortá Mór*) and the Penal Laws, with pictures of priests saying mass in the open air. The history course ended at 1916 and the Rising. The War of Independence and Civil War were too recent and divisive to be studied then, so quite a number of children left school unaware that there had been a civil war in Ireland.

Protestant children studied the same curriculum but often with a different perspective or bias. One Protestant girl remembered feeling that men like Wolfe Tone and Henry Joy McCracken (Protestant heroes of the 1798 Rising) 'belonged to us in a way that they could never belong to the Roman Catholic children'. Many students, looking back, came to feel that the history books – *Star Seanchas I* and *II* – were 'biased'. The Christian Brothers order had a reputation for teaching a strongly Anglophobic and sectarian version of Irish history. Like many subjects, history was often taught in Irish. One student recalled listening uncomprehendingly to his teacher and remembering only phrases such as '*Thanigh na Adventures go hÉireann*' (the adventurers came to Ireland) and '*Duirt T'ilkin Thómas*' (Silken Thomas said).

Maths

Arithmetic was another very important subject – known to many pupils as 'sums'. Children learned to chant their tables off by heart – and few ever forgot them: 'Three ones are three, three twos are six, three threes are nine,' etc. Having mastered tables, they learned how to add, subtract, and divide, to do fractions and compound interest. In a pre-calculator age, children were taught mental arithmetic. Whether they learned in English or Irish, this was something the pupils always remembered: 'At 12 we could do sums in our head for which many of today's Third Level students need a calculator.'

Geometry and trigonometry also featured on the curriculum, and the then currency of pounds, shillings and pence was mastered in that pre-decimal age. Using pencils (no biros or fountain pens), the children copied the sums into their sum copies – using a rubber to erase errors – or came up to the blackboard to work out fractions. 'We parroted numbers', one student recalled. 'Arithmetic and tables were a horror story – by constant repetition you eventually got the hang of them.'

English

English teaching again focused on grammar, syntax, punctuation and spelling. A Westmeath woman remembered that, in her school, 'English grammar was a speciality – three columns for general analysis and seven for particular analysis.' The pupils were also taught the moods and tenses of verbs. In senior class, children learned parsing and analysis. They would chant:

Common noun, masculine gender, third person, singular, no nominative case to the verb. Verb weak, transitive, indicative mood. Third person, singular, to agree with its nominative.

Poetry and prose also featured strongly on the English curriculum and many a child would still be able to recite off by heart the poems they learned decades after they had left the schoolroom behind them. The poets studied included Yeats, Shakespeare and Wordsworth. Shakespearean plays such as *The Merchant of Venice* featured on the curriculum for the senior classes. In one Midlands school, the principal would give the pupils a composition to do: 'If anyone produced a good phrase or a good paragraph, he would read it out to us and told us to remember that and put it into other compositions.'

Religious Education

Religious education involved learning prayers and Catechism – a typical question was 'Who made the world?'. One Sligo man remembered: 'The Catechism in those days we all learned off by heart. Quite a number of the answers, we hadn't a clue what they meant.' Children were taught the differences between venial and mortal sins, the circumstances under which it was permissible to do 'servile work' on the Sabbath, and other theological issues. Priests came into the schools from time to time to question pupils on their knowledge.

As well as the prayers and Catechism in class, children often found themselves spending up to two hours in church after Sunday mass for further instruction. The most popular Catechism used in primary schools was the Maynooth Catechism, popularly known as the Green Catechism. Protestant and Jewish children focused on studying the Scriptures. In schools where there were children belonging to minority faiths, the children were sent to the back of the room to study by themselves or to another room. One Protestant boy recalls his teacher, who was a priest, jokingly telling him to 'leave the room before we convert you'.

Other Subjects

In some schools, nature study was included on the curriculum, with pupils gathering around the teacher's desk to examine plants and flowers, or gathering minnows, tadpoles and other creatures in jars. A teacher from Co. Longford remembered the great excitement among her pupils when 'one year we produced one frog'.

Science was an optional subject which was taught in some schools but not in others.

Music and singing was also taught. Some children had the good fortune to have enthusiastic teachers who taught them songs in English and Irish. Many primary school children got to sing in church on Sundays and to take part in school choir competitions, liturgical festivals and other cultural events. In 1953, Sligo Feis (festival) marked its Golden Jubilee and the organisers praised 'The extraordinary strong support for the juvenile and junior classes. Children are becoming more *feis*-conscious.'

In the Juvenile Recitation for Girls event, there were eighty-nine competitors – an all-time record. The Kindergarten Cup competition had ninety-nine entrants. Teachers with an interest in the Irish language and music trained students for local, provincial and All-Ireland Feiseanna (festivals). In one school, the girls were encouraged to learn songs and to sing, but one child was beaten for singing an Elvis Presley song, which was considered blasphemous.

A report appeared in the *Irish Press* in the early 1950s on the Garryhill Flageolet Band in Co. Carlow, described as 'the only whistle band in the country' – with all the members under 14, and some as young as 9. The band uniforms were paid for by fundraising concerts. The uniform consisted of a green cap and blazer, cream skirt or trousers. There was a long waiting list to get into the band, with most of the children in the local school involved.

Art was included by some teachers in the curriculum, during the weekly half-day introduced by the

Department of Education in 1953, when teachers were permitted to teach subjects outside the prescribed curriculum. In 1955, the Council of Education recommended that drawing should be on the curriculum. National Art Competitions for children were organised from the middle of the decade, with the prizes being presented by politicians such as Dublin Lord Mayor, Robert Briscoe.

In January of 1955, a national art exhibition of work by national school children was staged in the National College of Art and Design. The exhibition included 10,000 pictures in pencil, pen, crayon and watercolours. Children from every county on the Island of Ireland took part. The biggest number of entries came from Connaught, with a reviewer writing that they showed 'a striking reflection of rural life in the west'. One professor at the National College noted sadly that 'so many of the children would never have the opportunity of continuing arts studies when they left school'.

Cooking, sewing and knitting were also primary subjects – usually for girls rather than boys, although there were some teachers who taught boys sewing in case they went for a career in the military or navy. One past pupil remembers sewing classes as:

> An exercise in mindboggling concentration. White calico, red thread, needle and a shiny table were the necessary prerequisites for perfect stitching, tacking, running, hemming and patching.

There were teachers who read stories such as *Huckleberry Finn* to their pupils. In a few schools there were libraries. The resources available to teachers were sometimes very poor. A teacher in a Midlands school, on taking up his post in his classroom, found the maps were out of date and there were no books that the children could read. He persuaded the school manager to buy new maps and some books.

Break Time

During the school day, classes generally lasted half an hour each – although Irish was allocated up to an hour a day. There was a half-hour lunch break between 12.30 and 1 p.m. Some children, particularly in urban areas, went home for lunch, but in country areas, the pupils generally went out to the school yard for their break.

Lunch was usually a couple of slices of bread and butter, with perhaps cheese and a piece of fruit such as an apple. Children often brought a bottle of milk with them to school. Some teachers provided the pupils with cocoa at break time. In one Midlands school, children were taught to thank their teacher in Irish for the cocoa, which she poured into the tin mugs they brought with them: '*Gur a maith agut, Bean Uí Raleigh, tá an cocoa go deas*' ('Thank you Mrs Raleigh, this cocoa is nice'). Milk was heated up in bottles placed before the school fire. Older children were given the job of boiling up a kettle for the cocoa or for the teachers' tea.

Children were also tasked with going to wells to get water or to collect cakes from neighbouring houses, or even to collect coal or sticks for the school fire. Ringing the school bell for the midday Angelus prayer was another job that pupils felt proud to be asked to do: 'For us at school, the Angelus signalled the completion of another half school day. Watches only belonged to the adult world.'

During the break, children played games in the school yard. Yards were usually separated by fencing or wire into areas for girls and boys. Many bishops felt that it was desirable to keep boys and girls segregated as much as practicable. Games such as 'Tig', skipping and hop-scotch, were played, and pupils also played sports such as hurley and Gaelic football or soccer during break time. If it was raining, children were still sent out if there was any shelter at all, such as a colonnade or a hut. During snowy weather, they went sliding up and down the yard or made snowmen.

School yards were often rough and stony, and grazed knees and elbows were a common occurrence as children slipped and fell. In some rural schools, the children could play in fields beside the school house. Looking back on his primary school days, one Westmeath man stated that two things stuck in his memory: 'the smell of the school toilets and the height of the nettles'. Dry toilets were a feature of a lot of school premises of the era and the nettle stings were dealt with through the application of dock leaves, the children learned a rhyme 'Dockers in, nettles out'.

Back in class at 1 p.m., the children continued their schooling until 3.30 p.m. when, to general delight, the ringing of the school bell signalled the end of the educational day. The homework given out usually included spellings, sums and compositions. The amount of homework given varied from teacher to teacher and school to school. In some places, it was considerable. Past pupils from one convent school recalled long evenings spent desperately trying to learn Irish spellings – knowing that they would be slapped if they did not know the correct spelling off by heart the following day.

Before leaving at the end of the day, pupils were given the chore of sweeping the classroom and tidying up the desks. When one girl learned on her way to school that there had been a fire in the building overnight, she panicked because she believed the fire was her fault. In her haste to get the job done, she thought she might have swept a little coal through a gap in the floorboards. Happily, the fire damage turned out to be minimal and no one was blamed for the incident.

For country children in particular, the journey home from school, especially in spring and summer, was a pleasant experience, an opportunity to play and explore. They waded through streams, drank beautifully pure water from wells and rivers, gathered apples, strawberries, blackberries, chestnuts, primroses and other flowers, climbed trees, ran, skipped, jumped and sometimes got invited into houses for milk and home-made bread or cakes. In Dublin, boys and girls gathered along the River Dodder or the canals to catch minnows in jam jars.

The walk home from school offered a chance for nature study and for extra exercise on top of the P.E. classes taught in many schools. It was not unusual, particularly in country areas, for children to walk four, 6 or 8 miles a day coming and going to school. Childhood obesity was not much of a health problem in 1950s Ireland.

School excursions were not common in Irish schools during this era. Resources for schools were not generous, and many parents would not have been able to pay for school outings. However, there were schools where such excursions did take place. Favourite destinations were Dublin Zoo and the airport. In one Midlands school, a penny a week was collected from each child throughout the school year to fund a trip by train to Dublin.

For children growing up far from the sea in a time when cars were rare, school trips gave them their first experience of the sea and of beaches. One child was completely stunned by the size of the Irish Sea at Howth. There were also occasions when schools were brought to see the circus or the Christmas pantomimes in Dublin or other theatres. As mentioned, school choirs were brought around the country to take part in music festivals and competitions.

Primary schools received visits from clergy, doctors and school inspectors from time to time. The clergy would usually visit to check on the religious knowledge imparted to the pupils and to prepare children for Holy Communion or Confirmation. Occasionally, bishops would visit as well, usually for events such as the opening of new buildings or classrooms or for school centenary or other significant anniversary occasions. Such days were an exciting break in the normal school routine, with the pupils lining up in their best clothes to greet the visiting dignitaries. There was often a special mass or service to mark the occasion. The celebrations were made even more special if a half-holiday was granted. In 1957, for example, a past pupil of St Mary's Christian Brothers school in Mullingar, Co. Westmeath, was appointed Abbot of Glenstal – one of the most prestigious positions in the Roman Catholic Church in Ireland. Dom Joseph Dowdall visited his alma mater, addressed the assembled pupils and ended his address by asking the school principal to cancel homework for the day and grant a half-holiday, which earned him a very enthusiastic reception.

The visit of the *Cigéra* (inspector) was generally unwelcome by staff and pupils alike. The inspector would sit in on classes and sometimes fire questions at pupils, with everyone afraid that they would let the side down by not knowing the answers. The inspectors checked the school registers and noted how many people were absent and what work was going on in the classroom.

Doctors and dentists were also unwelcome visitors, bringing unpleasant injections and big needles. In one primary school, the visiting dentist would actually extract teeth, and terrified children going into the room where he was working were greeted with the sight of a bucket filled with blood and discarded teeth.

School attendance inspectors checked that children were where they should be, and parents whose children were absent could find themselves receiving visits from the Gardaí. School attendance reports noted reasons given for absence. Illness was the main reason – or an illness of a parent. Reports for one school district gave the following reasons for pupil absenteeism: 'Child suffering from a sore throat', 'Child picking potatoes on father's farm', 'Boy got teeth extracted', 'Boy had mumps' and 'Mother was ill, the child had to look after the house'. It was often the case in country areas that boys would be absent to help with work such as turf cutting, gathering and harvesting.

Schools closed for big fairs such as the Athlone January Cattle Fair and the Ballinasloe Horse Fair. In the Midlands, children got a half-day when the Kilbeggan Races were on. In some schools, classes ended early on Pancake Tuesday, so that children could go home to feast on the pancakes before the rigours of Ash Wednesday and the forty days of Lent began. At Gainstown School in Co. Westmeath, the pupils would chant a song to their principal to remind him to finish school early: 'Dear Mr Moynihan, so friendly and kind. Don't let Pancake Night out of your mind.'

Pupils generally spent eight or nine years in primary school. Junior and senior infants and first year were followed by a move to 'the big room' and a new teacher. For boys in town schools, where different religious orders ran boys' and girls' schools, there was often an important rite of passage in which the boys would leave the care of the nuns and march to a boys' school run by Christian Brothers or some other religious order, chanting 'We're off to the Brothers' as they went.

Primary Certificate

In the final year of primary school, there was an examination known as the Primary Cert. 'The Primary', which was compulsory from 1943 until its abolition in 1962, was, for a majority of the generation of children who went through school in the 1950s, the only qualification they would get. Opinions differed on its usefulness, with some educational commentators considering it to be of little value while others believed it to be a quite demanding exam. Subjects taken included Irish, English and Arithmetic.

These were the sorts of questions that were asked in the Primary Cert exams:

1) Estimate the yield of turnips from a field of four acres, three roods and 16 square perches at the rate of 15 tons per acre.
2) Make out a shop bill for the following:
   a) 4½lb butter at 2*s* 8*d* per lb
   b) 3¼ stone of sugar at 2*d* per lb

c) 42 bottles of milk at 5½*d* each

d) 45 eggs at 4*s* 6*d* per dozen

e) 4lb of tobacco at 1*s* 10½*d* per oz

3) A man bought a house for £1,750. He let it for £120 per year, but had to pay out £41/£50 for the year in ground rent, rates, etc. What was his percentage profit on his outlay?

4) Say whether the words in italics are adjectives or pronouns:

a) Give me *that* book.

b) This pen is better than *that*.

c) *One* day you will be *one* of the world's workers.

5) Suits in a Dublin shop were marked in dollars for American visitors. One suit was marked £36 or $38.22c. What was the rate of exchange?

Armed with the Primary Cert, a majority of children finished their education as they turned 14. There was widespread unease about the fact that so many were leaving school for good at an age when they were still legally children. There were repeated calls for the school leaving age to be raised to 15 or 16 – particularly when the age went up to 15 in Great Britain and Northern Ireland. However, in 1954, the National Council on Education failed to recommend raising the age.

Some parents saw no value in education and wanted their children to be out earning money that was badly needed in so many impoverished households as the economy remained mired in recession. For many parents, a secondary education was simply beyond their means. One Cork woman remembered crying when she was told by her mother that she would have to leave school and get a job because there was no money to send her to the local convent secondary school:

> I said to my mother, 'I don't want to leave school,' but she said, 'I'm sorry, girl. We have no money, I couldn't send you anywhere. You'll have to leave school and you'll have to get a job.' And I'll always remember I was really and truly fed up, because there was nothing she could do, or I could do, to make extra money to go to secondary school.

However, as the 1950s went on, the numbers of children staying in the school system did steadily increase. Some primary schools had a seventh and even an eighth class. By 1959, there were 30,308 children in seventh class and 8,230 in eighth class. More secondary and vocational schools opened. A total of eighty-eight new secondary schools were built during the decade. From 48,559 pupils in second level education in 1950, the number had reached 73,431 by 1959.

3

Secondary School

The second-level education system in 1950s Ireland was divided into two main types of schooling. Firstly, there were vocational schools – commonly known as technical schools or 'Techs', where pupils were taught practical courses in subjects such as carpentry, mechanical drawing and typing or shorthand. These schools were under the management of Vocational Educational Committees in each county and city, and were the nearest 1950s Ireland got to providing multi-denominational education, although priests sat on the VECs.

Alternatively, there were secondary schools, which were nearly all run by Roman Catholic religious orders such as the Christian Brothers, Loreto Sisters, Mercy Nuns, Marist Brothers, Jesuits or Benedictines. There were also a number of Protestant schools, and there was a Jewish school in Dublin. Most secondary schools were single-sex. These schools all taught an academic curriculum aimed at providing pupils with qualifications that could secure them white collar jobs in banks, offices or the civil service, and which offered a path to university for a small number.

The curriculum for secondary students included Irish, English, Maths, Latin, Greek, French (or some other continental language such as German or Spanish), Science and Geography. There were two main exams on the secondary school cycle – the Inter Cert and the Leaving Cert. The Inter Cert – so called because it was midway between the Primary and Leaving Cert exams – was usually taken at the age of 15 or 16. The Leaving Cert, which was the gateway to third-level education, was taken two years later. There was no transition year at that time. The majority of pupils in both secondary and vocational schools left after the Inter Cert. An Inter Cert was enough to secure a job in the Civil Service.

Those who remained until the Leaving Cert were a truly privileged minority. In some secondary schools with 100 or more pupils, as few as five might sit the Leaving Cert in any year. In the academic year 1952–53, for example, a total of 51,151 pupils were enrolled in 447 secondary schools; 30,464 took the Inter Cert exam and just 12,687 students in the whole nation sat the Leaving Cert. By the 1959-60 school year, the numbers attending secondary schools had climbed to 73,431 and a total of 55,411 sat the Inter Cert. The Leaving Cert contingent was also up, but was still only 18,020.

The secondary school system reflected the huge class divide in Ireland at the time. While the national school educated:

> … the poor man's child alongside those from wealthier backgrounds, the secondary school was very largely the preserve of the middle class. Access to secondary schooling depended to a great extent on the ability of parents to pay what were often quite large fees. While some scholarships were available for those children hoping to attend secondary school, these scholarships were often very few in number.

As well as the secondary and vocational schools, there was also a curious hybrid known as a 'secondary top-up'. This was an extra two- or three-year cycle added on to primary school post Primary Cert, where children had a chance to study a range of subjects including science, domestic science and French, and could sit for the Inter Cert. Most of these secondary top-ups were attached to existing religious controlled schools where orders of brothers, nuns or priests were teaching primary children. In 1956–57 there were eighty-seven such schools in the country.

Pupils who attended the secondary top-ups had to travel elsewhere to sit their exams, as the secondary top-ups were not designated exam centres. An example of such a hybrid primary and secondary school was St Joseph's convent school in Rochfortbridge,

Co. Westmeath, where students were driven to Mullingar each day to sit the Inter Cert.

Many educationalists were critical of the secondary top-ups, seeing them as sub-standard and believing that they were operated by the religious orders in order to keep control over secondary education and to prevent the establishment of rival lay-run schools. But many of the religious orders – particularly the nuns – were anxious to provide equal educational opportunities and to try and keep their primary pupils in education past 14, if at all possible, and were aware that the demand for secondary schooling was there. Many secondary top-ups, including the one in Rochfortbridge, were given full recognition as secondary schools by the Department of Education during the 1950s.

The secondary schools of the era were fee-paying, which was one reason why few attended them, as many parents could not afford the fees. However, some schools charged relatively small fees, which were usually payable in two instalments – in September and January or in April and October (times of the year when farmers could be expected to make money at the fairs). Another reason for the low level of secondary schooling was the lack of schools. While the cities and larger towns usually had a number of such schools, many villages and country areas had no secondary or indeed technical school at all. A report stated that 'secondary school education was inaccessible to far too many and availed of by far too few.'

The provision of schools was slow to meet demand, and for many children, in a time when there was no school transport service and few families had cars, the secondary school was simply too far away. There were many cases where children who had walked 3 or 4 miles a day to primary school now cycled 10 or even more miles a day to secondary school. A few pupils travelled as many as 18 miles a day. Three pupils at the Mercy Convent, Trim, Co. Meath, battled daily through wind and rain to get to school from the village of Ballivor ten miles away, and one boy from Co. Roscommon cycled an incredible 40 miles a day to and from his secondary school in Co. Longford.

In a few areas, a transport system was organised. The Nuns of the Mercy convent in Longford reached an agreement with a local bus driver to collect and deliver pupils from across a wide area of the county. Other children were able to use the train, as the rail network, while contracting, was more widespread in the 1950s than today. In various parts of rural Meath in the early 1950s, pupils were collected by a station wagon from the nearest crossroads to their house.

Many of the secondary schools were boarding schools, and pupils came from a wide area. Boarding solved the problem of attending school for many children living too far away to walk or cycle home daily. One girl cycled 20 miles from Ballivor in Meath to Rochfortbridge in Westmeath to be interviewed by the school principal and finally enrolled – then she and her mother cycled home again. She began boarding in the school the following term.

In an era in which many children did not travel much beyond their home areas, secondary boarding school offered the first chance to meet youngsters from other parts of the country and hear different accents and dialects. A boy who arrived from Co. Kilkenny to board in the Carmelite College in Moate, Co. Westmeath, found that his accent and ways of pronouncing words was a source of endless fascination for the other pupils, and he in turn was amazed by the accents of the Midlands and the West.

The secondary schools of the 1950s were often quite austere places where discipline was strict. Corporal punishment was used in some schools. Central heating was usually unknown, and the strongest memory of many past pupils was the cold, which 'woke us up on our way to church'. As in many homes, chilblains were a common occurrence.

The normal pattern of the day went as follows for boarders: rise about 7 a.m., mass or service at 7.30 and breakfast at 8.15 – often eaten in silence with someone reading from some suitable spiritual work. Classes would begin at 9 a.m. and continue through to about 11.15, when there would be a fifteen-minute break. Dinner would take place at 1 p.m. with a short recreation period afterwards, followed by more classes from around 2 p.m. or 2.30 to 4 p.m. or 4.30. Tea was followed by two hours of supervised study and then prayers (usually the rosary in Catholic schools), then there was supper, followed by another hour of study, a short period of recreation, and bed around 9 p.m. or 9.30.

The meals served usually consisted of bacon and cabbage and parsnips for dinner, porridge and bread and butter for breakfast, and more bread and butter for supper. Drinks were milk, cocoa or Bovril; desserts were usually rice puddings or semolina, or something equally stodgy and unappetising. Custard and jelly or ice cream were rare treats. Many past pupils recalled being always hungry. One past pupil recalled how her years in boarding school taught her the importance of sharing – perfecting the skill of dividing a small chocolate bar into six or more tiny portions to share with friends, and also sharing small pieces of fish or meat. Chocolate bars or fruit in parcels from home were a hugely appreciated treat.

In some schools, pupils slept in large dormitories; in other schools they were allocated small cubicles with a basin, a bedside locker and sometimes a wardrobe. The students often washed in cold water, even in winter.

Secondary schools had uniforms, and these were usually purchased in Dublin, Cork or other big towns. The cost of uniforms was prohibitive for many parents, but, as with other clothes, the uniforms could be passed down from sibling to sibling. For those going to secondary school, wearing a uniform was a new experience, as very few primary schools had uniforms at that time. Sometimes that uniform created a barrier between secondary school children and their friends from primary school who were not continuing their education. In their eyes, the school blazers and ties and berets could appear way too 'grand and swanky'. In boarding schools the laundry was often done at weekends, sometimes by children in neighbouring industrial schools. One past pupil remembered 'the sight of lines of navy blue knickers, each bearing the name tag of their owner, exhibited in the breeze to dry'.

Boarders rarely went home for weekends. On Saturdays, sports such as hurling, camogie, rugby, cricket or hockey were played, and students were taken on supervised walks around the locality – recalled by one former convent pupil as 'be-hatted, be-gloved and in ladder-less black stockings, walking demurely two-by-two with eyes cast down'. There were no televisions in the schools then, so boarders spent their weekend leisure time reading, writing letters home or chatting. Some pupils recall the special treat of being allowed to listen to the All-Ireland finals on the radio if their county was playing, or playing records on a gramophone in the study hall. In some schools, sweets could be purchased, such as toffees known as 'dinky bars', which cost just 1p. At the St Louis convent in Dundalk there was a tuck shop that opened on Sundays, where pupils could buy toffee and small chocolate bars.

Curriculum

The secondary school curriculum focused mostly on languages, Maths and practical subjects such as cooking and science. There also tended to be a strong emphasis on team sports such as hurling, rugby, cricket or hockey. Irish was particularly important for those studying for the Leaving Cert, as a failure in Irish meant failing the entire exam. As with primary schools, some secondary schools taught the majority of subjects in Irish. English was also considered very important, with students studying poetry, prose and drama. Pupils could enter competitions such as the All-Ireland Irish Essay Contest, run by the Gaelic League, which attracted entrants from 236 schools in 1956. This competition encouraged high standards in written Irish and the chance to train for Irish language journalism.

Latin was taught in many schools and was important to know in an age when the Roman Catholic Mass was in Latin. The focus of study was usually the writings of Roman authors such as Livy, Virgil, Horace and Julius Caesar. The study of Latin was obviously important for those youngsters who went on to careers in medicine, pharmacy or the priesthood, but could have other unexpected uses as well. On a visit to Rome in 1950 for the Holy Year, some past pupils of a Christian Brothers secondary school were able to ask for directions in Latin from a priest when they got lost.

Classical Greek also featured in the curriculum in a number of schools. The most popular continental language taught in the secondary schools was French, possibly because so many of the religious orders running schools had historic connections to France – although only nine per cent of Leaving Cert students took the subject. There were few tape recorders available in schools until the end of the decade, however, so teachers and pupils were unaware of how the language actually sounded when spoken by native French people. As with Irish and English teaching, there was a strong emphasis on learning grammar and formal conversational French. Essay writing was given a great deal of attention in all language teaching.

German was taught in a few schools, but Spanish was not widely taught in the 1950s – an era before Spain became a number one holiday destination and Spanish children began coming to Ireland to study English (although students from a Madrid school did come to Dublin for two months in 1956, staying in Belvedere College). Just two students took Leaving Cert Spanish in 1952, and both failed.

There was often a gender bias in the subjects offered. While girls and boys alike studied languages and maths, some schools only allowed boys to study science and only girls to study domestic science:

Girls were pushed towards Pass Maths rather than Honours for Inter Cert. Irish education in the fifties did tend to see boys as being educated towards careers as doctors, lawyers, engineers or mechanics, while girls were seen as progressing towards careers in nursing, teaching or the religious life – as well as being trained up for their 'natural function' as housewives and mothers.

A conference of secondary school teachers in 1952 heard that it was important to train girls for their future roles as wives and mothers. However, this was not the case in every school. Many convent schools did want their girls to follow whatever career they wished, and taught chemistry, biology and physics as well as the domestic sciences of cooking and sewing. Girls in secondary school outperformed boys in the Inter and Leaving Cert exams in every year in the 1950s. More girls sat the Inter Cert than boys, but the reverse was the case at Leaving Cert level. Only about a third of secondary schools, however, taught science at all, and many schools had no science labs. Government expenditure on science education was among the lowest in Europe.

Secondary schools often invested much time in music and drama. Pupils got the chance to develop acting or singing talents in musicals. For example, the Meath Diocesan junior seminary, St Finian's College in Mullingar, staged annual productions of Gilbert and Sullivan musicals such as *The Pirates of Penzance*, with younger boys playing the female roles. Rockwell College staged *The Yeoman of the Guard* in 1955.

Choirs from schools such as Our Lady's Bower, Athlone, Convent of Mercy, Enniscorthy, and Good

Counsel College, New Ross, among many others, performed in choir festivals and in major cultural celebrations such as the annual Tostál Festival. Many schools offered pupils the opportunity to play musical instruments such as the piano or harp, and some former pupils had very fond memories of dedicated teachers teaching them religious, folk, traditional and even pop songs.

Sport also featured in the secondary school curriculum. Some schools focused mostly on PE or 'drill', but many played Gaelic football, hurling, rugby, cricket or hockey. The fiercely nationalistic Christian Brothers concentrated solely on Gaelic sport – particularly football. The Presentation Brothers in Cork and the Jesuits at Blackrock College, on the other hand, focused on rugby.

Convent schools tended to play hockey or tennis, although camogie was also popular. There was no women's Gaelic football then, nor did girls play rugby or soccer. Some schools, such as the Carmelite College in Moate, became veritable sporting powerhouses.

From the middle of the decade, new sporting competitions in Gaelic games such as the Hogan Cup (hurling) and the Cusack Cup (football), offered secondary school pupils opportunities to compete for sporting medals, and built on the work being done for primary school pupils with the Cumann na mBunScol competition, which promotes engaging in Gaelic games in primary schools.

Secondary schools got the opportunity to go on excursions to various parts of the country – such as the Kerry Gaeltacht and the Dail – and even overseas.

In May 1955, pupils from each Marist Brothers School went by plane, boat and train to Rome to take part in the Beatification Ceremonies for the founder of the order.

The pupils who were fortunate enough to make it into secondary school were aware that they were the lucky ones, and that their parents or working older siblings were making sacrifices to educate them. They tended to work hard, appreciative of the opportunity. For day pupils, a long day in the classroom was often followed by chores on the farm or in a family-run shop when they came home, before doing a couple of hours of homework.

For some children, the secondary school experience was a happy one, with dedicated and inspiring teachers and long-lasting and close friendships and a broadening of horizons. For others, however, it was a bleak experience to be endured, with harsh and authoritarian teachers. For most secondary school students, schooldays were probably neither the happiest nor the most miserable days of their lives but a mixture of good and bad experiences that the majority of children of the era did not get the chance to have.

Pupils in secondary schools were encouraged to see themselves as future leaders in all walks of society, be it in the church, law, government or other professions. In the elite Gonzaga College, Co. Dublin, one boy recalled how, whenever they were misbehaving in the classroom or the study, one teacher would shout at them, 'In twenty years' time, you'll be running this country – who else can run it?'

The children who went to secondary school usually emerged with a strong sense of self-confidence, which was not always the case with primary school students.

A poem by pupils in St Louis's secondary school, Multyfarnham, Westmeath, sets out the feelings of the pupils on their return from holidays to the school grind in 1955:

Our holidays are spent and done
And back to Multy we have come
With spirits low and feelings mixed
To rise once more at half past six
We go, alas, back into class,
To swot at Irish, Greek and Maths.
And listen daily to professors
Or answer back or 'No Sir', 'Yes Sir.'
You feel you'd rather be at home
Or lie upon the rack;
Not start to study Ancient Rome
On the first Sunday back.
Why do they make us study hard?
When it's so nice and sunny?
But that's the way they do things here
Now don't that strike you funny?
Do they not know our hearts are sad?
That love of work we lack?
Our lot is very dull, my lad
On our first Sunday back.

Vocational Schools

The vocational schools attracted increasing numbers of students throughout the 1950s. Boys and girls attended day classes as second-level students, while some youngsters who had finished school after Primary Cert returned to education to attend night classes in the 'Techs'. There was demand for such schools, and dozens opened during the decade or expanded their existing facilities.

Between 1951 and 1954, the education minister was Sean Moylan, described by a colleague as 'that self-educated and cultured carpenter'. Moylan was himself a former vocational school teacher. Although he once remarkably declared that he 'did not believe in equal opportunities for all', he did wish to see vocational schooling expand. During his term as minister, 160 new schools were provided and 20,000 students were attending full-time courses by 1954.

By 1959, there were 17,334 girls and boys under 16 attending vocational schools. The day pupils generally did a two-year course, ending with what was known as the Group Cert. The subjects taught included Irish, English, maths, woodwork, cookery, needlework, rural science and mechanical drawing. The Group Cert qualification enabled boys and girls to:

> … enter trades such as carpenters, plumbers, plasterers, block layers, painters and electricians, as well as

obtaining apprenticeships in semi-state companies such as the ESB, Bord Na Mona and CIE.

Girls qualified for secretarial and other office employment, as well as areas of service and factory work.

As in the secondary schools, there were fixed ideas about which subjects were most appropriate for boys or girls. Boys were rarely given the opportunity to study domestic science, while girls were excluded from carpentry, mechanical drawing and rural science. As in the secondary schools, girls were steered towards pass maths and had a lower pass standard than boys. Across the whole system, there was an attitude that girls don't do honours maths or science. Girls were also excluded from vocational craft courses.

There was an anxiety in some quarters that the vocational and secondary schools, in the words of the Rev Felim O'Brien, should not forget 'the fundamental function of a woman' (to be a mother and homemaker). A Westmeath priest felt that the schools were failing to teach domestic science skills – exclaiming that 'the shyness of the young man to marry' was due to 'the inability of the young women of the country to cook properly'. Ireland had one of the lowest marriage rates in the world at the time.

Girls attended vocational schools in equal numbers to boys and were eager to study and acquire skills and qualifications. The CEO of the Co. Westmeath VEC, Michael O'Boyle, spoke with pride of the high standards obtained by girls in secretarial courses, how well qualified they were, and how highly regarded by job interview panels.

Although there was often a snobbish attitude, especially in small-town Ireland, towards the children who went to 'The Tech', many of the pupils enjoyed their schooling there – especially after the harshness so many had endured in primary school. For a majority, vocational school delayed by two or three years the inevitable departure to a working life in Britain. As a memo to the government noted:

> The type of girl who in pre-war days would normally seek factory work on leaving primary schools is now attending VEC classes and qualifying for jobs as a cleric or shorthand typist etc. Some girls are getting more attractive jobs in commercial offices or are going to Britain.

Schooling Abroad

The massive emigration from Ireland in the 1950s involved mostly adults and teenagers, but whole families sometimes left the country together. For the children who were taken to Britain or America, schooling was sometimes not a great deal different from Ireland. Many immigrant children in Britain were brought up in little Irish enclaves in places like Manchester, Birmingham, London or Coventry. The teachers in the primary schools were quite often nuns, brothers or priests from Ireland. Corporal punishment was as much a feature of school life in Britain as in Ireland. At Mass on Sundays, the priests were usually Irish. There were GAA (Gaelic Athletic Association) clubs and Irish language and dancing classes.

The only differences from Ireland were that secondary schooling was free, the school leaving age was a year higher (15), and the 11+ exam offered a number of working-class Irish-born children, and the children of Irish immigrants, a path into grammar school and an opportunity to get to university and enter the middle class. Connections with home were kept up through summer visits to grandparents and other relatives, but few would return permanently to Ireland.

Other children were taken to America. Here, again, they often found themselves growing up in Irish-Catholic districts in cities such as Boston and New York, where, as in Britain, they were educated in religious schools where the teachers were nuns, priests and brothers – particularly nuns – who moved to America in large numbers in the 1950s to found new schools across the country. The teachers saw it as their job to help integrate the immigrant children into American society and worked to eradicate the Irish brogues and turn their charges into American-accented boys and girls.

Unlike in Britain, Irish children in America, in the pre-jet plane era, did not often return on holiday, but Irish-born teachers and priests, as well as classes in Irish music, dance and sport, kept them connected in some way to the land they had come from and which had so little to offer them.

Unlike twenty-first-century Ireland, the schools of 1950s Ireland – both primary and secondary – were not multicultural places. An occasional child with an American or British accent was an exotic rarity, a mixed-race child (like singer Phil Lynott) even rarer still. In some parts of the Midlands, the nearest thing to cultural or linguistic diversity in the classroom was provided by the children known as 'The Westies' or '*Gaeltacht*'. These were the children of small farmers from Connemara and Mayo, who were brought up from their impoverished livings on the Western seaboard to new farms on former big house estates acquired and divided by the Land Commission. The accents of these children were strange to the ears of their new schoolmates and, even more unusual, they sometimes spoke Irish.

Many of the 'Westies' long remembered the experience of leaving their homes and schools on a Friday, watching as their names were struck off the school rolls and as their neighbours and relatives, some crying, lined up to wave them goodbye. A long journey by bus or train followed to their new homes. They settled down in the Midlands and attended new schools, and were happy for the most part, it seems. But many always had a sense that they remained outsiders.

When the Irish-speaking Blasket Islanders were moved to the Kerry mainland in 1953, there was one child amongst them: Gearóid Cheaist Ó Catháin. The National Press reported how, 'The little boy played and laughed and shouted with the others, entirely unaware that in a language he does not understand he had won headlines in the newspapers as "The loneliest boy in the world."'

An Tostál

The Tostál festivals, held annually between 1953 and 1958, were major cultural events, aimed at showcasing Irish culture and welcoming tourists to the country. The word *tostál* means 'pageant'. Tens of thousands of people took part in events such as spectacular pageants on the hills of Tara and Slane, where St Patrick's lighting of the first Easter Fire was re-enacted. There were military parades, drama festivals, arts and crafts exhibitions, sports tournaments and many other festivals in cities and towns across the nation. The Tostál would lead to the setting up of the Tidy Towns Competition, the Rose of Tralee Festival and the Dublin Theatre Festival over the following decade.

Children took part in the Tostál all across the country. In 1954, the Abbeyleix Bonham Girls' Tin Whistle Band and the Bonham School of Dancing participated in the Tostál Parade. In Mullingar, Westmeath, Tostál celebrations included a children's fancy dress *céilí*, while in Newport, Mayo, Cullmore Children's Pipe Band played a selection of Irish airs in a variety show. In Westport,

Mayo, a *Tostál Na nÓg* was formed with a membership of fifty boys, all under 16. During the festival, they helped run events and acted as tour guides. A prize was awarded to the first boy to speak for five minutes in Irish to a member of the town's Tostál organising committee, 'and as the boy will not know which member is selected for the purpose of awarding this prize, there should be plenty of Irish spoken during the week'.

Tostál week 1954 in Westport also included a regatta for boys under 16 on the river, a roller skating championship on the Mall, and a fishing competition in the Demense of Westport House.

In Virginia, Co. Cavan, in 1954, the Tostál parade included the Virginia School Harmonica Band, which comprised forty boys and girls marching three deep, with the girls dressed in Tostál costume and the boys wearing white shirts with gold and maroon sashes.

In Kilkenny, crowds attending Tostál festivities in the castle were entertained by the De La Salle Boys' Fife and Drum Band from Ballaghadreen, Co. Roscommon. The Tostál parade in Limerick included the local Catholic Boy Scouts troop. There was much praise in the local press for the 'Crown of Glory' pageant, which was staged by pupils of the Presentation Convent as part of the Tostál and of the Marian year. One reviewer stated that he was 'wonderfully impressed, by the beauty and excellence' of the production: 'Our Lord and Our Lady must have been very pleased with the little ones who represented "them" to others.'

Limerick also staged a special children's art exhibition. In Waterford, the Tostál Parade in 1954 included St Declan's Girls' Pipe Band.

During the 1953 Tostál, some places had a Children's Day on Easter Monday – La Na nÓg. In Bray, Co. Wicklow, the girls' choir from the local technical school performed a concert of Irish songs. In Cashel, Co. Tipperary, the Tostál parade included the local Christian Brothers School Boys' Flageolet Band. The Mallow, Co. Cork, parade included the Flageolet Band of the local Patrician schools. During the Kells Tostál, 13-year-old Florrie Jordan, who was dressed in national costume, 'declaimed the Tostál message in Irish'.

In Dun Laoghaire, the Tostál of 1953 included a production of *Land of Heart's Desire* performed by the local children's theatre.

At the 1955 Tostál in Cork, a choir of 500 children sang the national anthem and 'A Nation Once Again' before an audience of thousands, including the then-Taoiseach John Costello. Newspapers commented that 'an attractive feature of the Cork parade was the participation of 1,000 city school children in the distinctive outfits of their schools and colleges, half a dozen of which had also provided Flageolet and Percussion Bands'. At the Dun Laoghaire Tostál parade, the participants included Arklow Cuman Na nÓg, the Catholic Boy Scouts and Arklow Flageolet Band.

During the three weeks of An Tostál events in Cork city, a concert took place in the Savoy cinema at which the accordion band of St Joseph's School, Mardyke, 'played a number of stirring Irish airs and popular tunes with remarkable skill'. At the same event, Bulcaden Boys' and Girls' Tin Whistle Band from Co. Limerick played to great acclaim and South Monastery School Percussion Band 'won the hearts of the audience' with a delightful selection. The talented pupils of Presentation Convent Bandon also presented a very colourful historical pageant.

4

Toys and Games

Irish children in the 1950s grew up in a world in which frugality was the norm and most families had little money for expensive toys. The toys and games children received were often handed down from older siblings or were home-made. But, children then were inventive and adventurous, and got much out of the toys they had. A wide variety of games were played in the schoolyard and in the home. Children also had perhaps more freedom than later generations. They were allowed – indeed almost expected – to play outside if the weather was dry and to wander long distances. With few cars on the roads, it was safe for children to play on country roads and town streets. The singer Joe Dolan remembered the excitement on the rare occasions that a car appeared on the road outside his home. Someone would shout 'ACC!' ('A car coming!') and the vehicle would be watched with interest.

The first toys young children received, as infants, were usually soft toys such as teddy bears or rag dolls. Toys were made out of matches, bits of wood, paper bags, straw, cork and other materials. Twigs and small branches could provide the materials for catapults, whistles, pop guns and spinning sticks. One woman remembered how her father, who was a tailor, would use the scraps and clippings left over from his work to make 'little rag dolls, bunny rabbits and dogs' as presents for little ones whose parents could not afford presents of toys.

Wooden spools with a piece of twine through them also made simple toys. Pretty much anything that could be used to fashion a toy was utilised by parents and children. A small box could be transformed into a doll's bed and furniture for the dolls' house could be crafted by a parent or a neighbour. One doting grandfather made a beautiful dolls' house – a mini version of his own house – for his 5-year-old granddaughter. She still had it sixty years later.

Balls could be made from a variety of materials. Sometimes children playing football were wary of breaking panes of glass and attracting severe punishment. This problem could be resolved by getting the local butcher to provide a pig or sheep's bladder, or by using paper and string. A 'crolly', or rag doll, was also very popular: the doll came with an outfit and extra clothes could often be made up at home. Wooden building bricks were popular in many homes and were not expensive. Paint sets, crayons and pencils, and balloons were other easily obtained

presents. Boys were encouraged to wear cowboy outfits and toy guns, while girls were given nurses' outfits.
Simple wind-up toy animals such as monkeys, dogs and
giraffes were also popular, as were toys on wheels.

For most children, toys were very simple. 'We didn't
really have a lot of toys,' one man remembered. 'You'd
make animals from corks and bits of sticks, and balls from
paper and string. We also used inner parts of disused clocks
to make spinning tops.' Dressing-up boxes made for an
enjoyable time when it was too wet to go out and play.
The box might include scarves, hats, dresses, shirts, curtains,
high-heeled shoes, necklaces, and handbags – anything that
wasn't used any more but could be used in a game.

Board games played by children included Ludo, Snakes
and Ladders and Dominos. For older children, Scrabble
became popular after its introduction in the mid 1950s,
and Lego first appeared in the shops in 1958. The toy
whistle and the wooden catapult were features of out-
door play, and some children also enjoyed roller skating,
while old prams and boxes could be converted into
go-karts. The toy shops advertised more elaborate and
expensive toys that not all children could afford at the
time. These included Hornby railway sets and mechanical sets, Dinky and Corgi cars. There were dolls that
could talk and walk and had what were rather weirdly
described as 'flirting' eyes.

Toys were divided according to gender: boys were
offered toy trains, lorries and cars and other mechanical
objects, while girls were offered dolls, toy prams, toy

sewing machines, kitchen sets and even toy pastry machines. Cowboy outfits were generally reserved for boys too. An *Irish Independent* competition for children offered a 'Davy Crockett outfit' as the first prize. Among the more expensive toys on sale at Christmas 1953 in Dublin shops were a child's typewriter at 36/11*s*, a toy cash register at 38/6*s*, a 'little princess' doll at 61*s*, a toy fort at 39/6*s*, and a dolls' house at 50*s*. Woolworths stores, of which there were many in Ireland, sold a wide variety of toys at much cheaper prices. These included toy tanks, model cars, plasticine, Airfix construction sets, polo sticks, hula hoops, frisbees, and mechanical car sets known as Scalextric.

During the 1950s, toy-making technology advanced, with toys increasingly made from plastic or synthetic fibres, although there was still a market for wooden handcrafted toys as well.

On the streets and in the school playground, children played a wide variety of games. 'Tig' was one of the favourites, as was hide-and-seek. Using a piece of chalk to mark out squares, children could play the ever popular game of hopscotch, or 'beds' as it was known in some areas. Another game, known as 'Jacks', involved throwing pebbles in the air four or five at a time, to be caught or picked up. One of the most popular games was marbles: children collected and exchanged these, often playing with them in the gutter. Writer Desmond Ellis recalled how old bicycle wheels could be transformed into hoops and how he and his friends 'went on Dinky car safaris through the dense jungle of the long grass'.

A simple rope could provide a swing, often attached to lampposts or trees, and in winter an old wooden box would be transformed into a sleigh. Skipping was particularly popular; the most skilled could not just avoid getting their feet entangled in the rope but could turn around in mid-air. Boys generally regarded girls at being better at skipping than they were. The skipping ropes could be very heavy, with one child remembering being 'knocked out on one occasion when hit by the rope, which was being turned at great speed'.

Popular playground games included 'Red Rover'. This involved six to ten, or more, children forming two opposing lines, with those in each line all clasping hands. One team would send a runner towards the opposing team, who would try to crash in between the other team's players where their hands met. The defending team tried to stop the attack and capture the runner. If the runner broke through, they grabbed a player from the other team and took them back to join their team. If he didn't break through, he was captured by the other team. As the game proceeded, the players would chant 'Red Rover, Red Rover, send someone over'. A variation of this game was Bulldog, in which two lines of children would face each other and one line would then charge fast and hard against the opposite line, seeking to break through it.

Another game called 'O'Grady says' involved one child calling out commands to the other children in the group, such as 'O'Grady says "Stand on one leg"' or 'O'Grady says "Touch your toes"'. A variation of this game was, 'Mother may I?' where one player would 'exercise Mother powers' of 'Mother, may I turn around', etc. 'O'Grady says' is the Irish variation of the popular game 'Simon says'.

Walls could be climbed or walked along, and could also be used for balancing against when doing handstands, which girls were considered to be particularly good at. Children bounced balls off the walls, sometimes two at a time, while chanting rhymes such as 'Aleri':

One, two, three, aleri
Four, five, six, aleri
Seven, eight, nine, aleri
Ten, aleri, catch the ball

'Piggy in the middle' involved one child standing in the middle of a circle as 'Piggy'. The other players would throw the ball to one another over Piggy's head until they managed to catch the ball, at which point the child who threw the ball became Piggy.

As children ran, skipped, jumped and threw balls against walls, they chanted rhymes. There were numerous rhymes, including the following:

Teddy Bear, teddy bear, turn around
Teddy bear, teddy bear, touch the ground
Teddy bear, teddy bear, go upstairs
Teddy bear, teddy bear, say your prayers
Teddy bear, teddy bear, switch off the light
Teddy bear, teddy bear, say goodnight
Goodnight, teddy bear, goodnight

A-hunting we will go
A-hunting we will go
We'll catch a fox
And put him in a box
And never let him go

Here we go round the sponge ball,
the sponge ball, the sponge ball
Here we go round the sponge ball,
on a cold and frosty morning

One potato, two potato, three potato, four,
Five potato, six potato, seven potato More!

I made you look, I made you stare
I made the barber cut your hair
He cut it long, he cut it short
He cut it with a knife and fork

She sells seashells on the seashore

I scream, you scream, we all scream for ice cream

And one that was probably not chanted round the schoolyard:

Our school is a very good school
It's made of sticks and plaster
The only thing that's wrong with it
Is the baldy master

The pain of gum boils, which were a common affliction among children then, when many suffered poor nutrition and little dental care due to poverty, led to a rhyme that went as follows:

> If a gum boil could boil oil
> How much oil could a gum boil boil
> If a gum boil could boil oil

Other rhymes included 'Oranges and Lemons' and 'Ring a Ring o' Roses'. Children singing 'Oranges and Lemons' would form a circle, with two children at a time dancing under an arch made by the other children's upraised arms.

> Oranges and lemons, say the bells of St Clement's
> You owe me five farthings, say the bells of St Martin's
> When will you pay me? say the bells of Old Bailey
> When I grow rich, say the bells of Shoreditch
> When will that be? say the bells of Stepney
> I do not know, says the great bell of Bow
>
> Here comes a candle to light you to bed
> Here comes a chopper to chop off your head
> Chop, chop, chop, chop, the last one is dead

> Ring a ring o' roses
> A pocket full of posies
> A-tishoo! A-tishoo! We all fall down

Cows in the meadows
Eating buttercups
A-tishoo! A-tishoo!
We all jump up

A detergent called Rinso provided a chant to accompany the bouncing of a rubber ball against a wall:

Plainy packet of Rinso
Over packet of Rinso
Doyny packet of Rinso
Right leg packet of Rinso
Left leg packet of Rinso
Backy packet of Rinso

Plainy is an underhand throw of the ball, over is an outward throw, Doyny is where the ball hits the ground before it hits the wall, and right leg is where it is bounced under the leg.

Play/Games/Rhymes

Queenie I-0

One child is picked to be 'Queenie', and that person turns their back to everyone else. She then throws the ball over her shoulder. Everyone else tries to catch the ball and the one who catches it shouts 'caught ball'. They are now 'on'. However, if nobody catches the ball, whoever picks it up hides it behind their back. Everyone else also put their hands behind their backs, and they sing to Queenie:

> Queenie, Queenie, who's got the ball?
> Are they short, or are they tall?
> Are they hairy, or are they bald?
> You don't know, because you don't have the ball

Queenie then has to guess who has the ball through a process of elimination. If the person with the ball is the last one to be picked, then that person becomes Queenie and the game starts over again.

A version of the rhyme 'Queenie' was used by Paul McCartney in his 2013 song 'Queenie Eye'. McCartney played the game as a child growing up in a Liverpool Irish family in the 1950s.

My Lord Luke and My Lord John

In this chant and game, two players face each other and join their hands, forming an arch. The other players form a line and proceed under the arch. As they go they chant, 'My Lord Luke and my Lord John, let everybody pass but the very last man.' As the last 'man' goes through, the arch drops and tries to trap him. If it succeeds, that player lines up behind one of the players forming the arch. The game continues until all have been 'captured'.

Single and Chain Tig

In single Tig, one person is chosen as 'it'. They then have to run after the other players. When one of the players is touched, the person who is 'it' shouts out, 'Tig'. The player touched then takes over as 'it' and chases after the others. The game ends when everyone has been caught.

Chain Tig is a variation on this, in which two players with hands joined chase after the others. When a player is 'Tigged' they join the first two in a chain, which grows until all have been caught. One man remembered how playing Tig was a great way to get warm during break before returning to his chilly, poorly heated rural classroom.

Carry a Lady to London

This was another rhyme chanted as children raced through arches:

> Give me a pin to stick in my thumb
> To carry a lady to London
> Give me another to stick in my other
> To carry her a little bit further

Fox and Hounds

Fox and Hounds was popular among country children. One child is 'Fox' and goes into hiding among the bushes and trees. The other players are the hounds and chase after the 'fox'.

Dogs and Rabbits was a variation on this. Different areas of the playground are marked off as burrows.

Those playing the rabbits have to race from one burrow to another through the players who are dogs. If a dog catches a rabbit, they then becomes a rabbit and have to race for the burrow. A dog cannot touch the rabbit if they reach the burrow, but if the rabbits are cowardly and don't chance racing the dogs by running from burrow to burrow, then the leader of the dogs could shout, 'Come on lads, we'll bolt them.' Then the dogs attack the burrow and throw out the rabbits.

Jackstones

This was one of a number of games played by children involving stones. It was based upon the ability of the player to juggle two stones with one hand and pick up the remaining stones off the ground while the juggled stones were in the air.

Another variation required the player to put one hand flat on the ground and to place stones in various patterns around it with their free hand, again while the remaining stones were in the air. The stones used often came from the seaside.

Dog and Cat

The 'dog' is a long rod about 2ft long with a point at one end. The 'cat' is a rod 6in long with points at each end. This is put sitting across two stones and from there is pitched away as far as possible using the dog. It is then thrown back by the other player. The cat is then 'catted', which involves hitting one of the pointed ends of it, lifting it off the ground and hitting it as far as possible and repeating this up to three times. The winner is the player who gets the 'Cat' as far away as possible.

The playwright Bernard Farrell recalls a similar game called Dab, which was played by two boys. Each boy threw a coin against a wall and the boy whose coin ended closest to it became the 'killer'. The victim had to throw his coin as far as possible; the 'killer' aimed for it with his own coin; if he hit it he would win it.

Dusky Bluebells

Dusky Bluebells was another game, described by Deirdre Purcell in her book *Follow Me Down to Dublin*. Played by girls, it involved the children forming a circle and holding hands at head height, with one girl chosen to dance through the raised hands. The children would chant:

> In and out go the dusky bluebells
> In and out go the dusky bluebells
> In and out go the dusky bluebells
> We are the masters
> Tararappa, rappa, rappa
> On my shoulder
> Tararappa, rappa, rappa
> On my shoulder
> Tararappa, rappa, rappa
> You are the chosen

The girl walking or dancing through the circle would then stop and put her hand on the shoulder of the girl in front of her. This girl would then join the first girl in the middle of the circle and grasp her by the hips conga-style, and the dance and chant would begin again. The game would continue until there was just one girl left to be chosen, or the length of the conga left no room to move.

In another game, two girls would make an arch by raising their joined hands above their heads. All the other players would then march around the two, passing under the arch in pairs while chanting:

Here's the robbers
Passing by, passing by
Here's the robbers passing by
My fair lady
What did the robbers
Do to you?
Do to you?
Do to you?
What did the robbers
Do to you
My fair lady?
Stole my watch
Stole my chain
Stole my chain
Stole my chain
Stole my watch and stole my chain
My fair lady

The arch was then brought down, trapping the girl who was underneath it. She was then asked to choose one of the others, and stood behind the girl of her choice, holding onto her hips. The game would continue until there was only one participant left to go under the arch.

Another song and dance involved girls joining hands in a circle and singing:

> Wallflowers, wallflowers growing up so high
> We're all pretty maidens that never want to die
> Especially (one child in the group would then be named)
> She is the only one
> O, fie, for shame, O, fie, for shame
> Turn your back against the game

Moving with the circle, the named child, turning her back, held hands backwards. The game continued until everyone was named, had turned and was dancing backwards.

Broken Statues was a game in which children stood in a line and 'someone came to you, spun you around and cast you away. You stumbled and whatever way you ended up, you had to freeze and couldn't move.'

The 1950s were a time of political instability, with three general elections in six years and three changes of government. Although few children would have had any interest in politics, they did enjoy chanting political rhymes, like the following, which referenced Fianna Fáil Leader Éamon De Valera and his Fine Gael opponent John Costello:

Vote, vote, vote for De Valera
In comes Cost-ello at the door-i-o
Costello is the one
That'll have a bit of fun
And we don't want De Valera anymore-i-o

The writer Alice Taylor remembers a rhyme she learned from the woman who did the Monday laundry in her home, which went as follows:

Big fleas have little fleas
Upon their backs to bite them
And little fleas have littler fleas
And so on infinitum

Those brought up in cities and towns saw the streets as 'our playgrounds', the streets were safer to play on compared to nowadays as there were fewer cars. In Sligo and other towns, boys played football with paper balls. In one Midlands village, 'a sort of game of cricket was played'. Playing skittles was also very popular with boys and girls.

For those living near the sea, Sunday afternoons and summer holidays brought trips to the beach – long afternoons spent building sandcastles, kicking a ball around and drawing in the sand. In some cities and towns, councils provided playgrounds with swings, slides and other attractions. For country children, summer days and walks home from school brought opportunities to play Cowboys and Indians, Soldiers, and Hide-and-Seek in fields and woods, as well as climbing trees and learning to swim in local rivers or lakes.

Children were expected to stay outdoors all day if it was dry, only coming home for meals and bed. If they fell out of trees or cut their knees, that was seen as an occupational hazard of play – knees were often stained purple where iodine had been applied to cuts! Children with bicycles could spend their days travelling long distances playing and exploring. Two brothers from Cavan town and their friends routinely cycled down into Westmeath and Meath and up as far as the Fermanagh border, playing Pirates on an island along the River Erne, Hide-and-Seek in the woods on the Farnham Estate, and, in winter time, constructing a sleigh and tobogganing down Tullymongan Hill in Cavan town.

In suburban South Dublin, children gathered along the Dodder with glass jars or bottles to catch minnows, which would then be used as bait when they went fishing. In Dublin, when children wanted to end a game, they would shout out, 'All in, all in, the game is broke up.'

A popular hobby among children was to collect 'chaneys'. Chaneys were pieces of china, delph and glass that could be found in newly ploughed fields or sometimes in building sites. Children used the often brightly coloured pieces in games.

When the winter weather and dark nights kept children indoors, they played a variety of games. 'We made our own amusements,' one woman remembered of her childhood in a house devoid of radio, TV or electricity.

Games like Shop or Doctors and Nurses could be played with an assortment of boxes, papers, cups and saucers and other household objects. Dominos, Snakes and Ladders and Ludo were popular board games. Some children learned to play chess. Crayons and paper enabled children to enjoy drawing, and paintboxes for children were also available. Boxes, blankets and chairs could be transformed into a castle.

Halloween games enjoyed by children included ducking for apples in a basin or bucket of water, or trying to take a bite from an apple hanging on a string, while keeping your arms behind your back. Trick-or-treating as it now exists was not common then, but children did dress up in costumes and had great fun gathering nuts: 'It took all our climbing skills to conquer the trees – we climbed to the top and then out as far along the swaying branches as we dared.' Back home on Halloween, which some children called Snap Apple Night, the nuts were cracked with a stone on the flagstone before the fire, while apples were suspended from cords tied to meat hooks on the rafters of the kitchen or floated in a tub or basin in the middle of the floor. Children would go out and 'lift gates', or ring doorbells before running away.

On 26 December, St Stephen's Day, there was another opportunity for children to dress up and go door to door as 'Wren boys' – hunting the wren and chanting the song:

The wren, the wren, the king of all birds
St Stephen's Day he's caught in the furze

Up with the kettle, down into the pan
Tuppance or Truppence to burn the wren
All silver and no brass, give us our silver and let us pass

Playing conkers was a popular game in the autumn. Hours could be spend collecting them, and in some areas there were conker championships, the object being 'to smash your rivals' conkers with your own', as Deirdre Purcell recalls it. The matches tended to be 'short and brutal'. Conkers on strings were a familiar sight in school play yards and streets around the country. No one worried too much about eye injuries.

Cowboys and Indians was a favourite game all year round. Toy guns with a roll of caps and a holster constituted the 'Holy Grail' of toys, according to playwright Bernard Farrell, 'You used to turn the holster the wrong way so you could draw to the front, foxing the other fella.' If a toy gun wasn't to hand, imagination could kick in:

If you hadn't a gun, you'd use a hurley for a rifle, or the branch of a tree, and you'd be riding into town, slapping your own behind as though it was the horse's behind, you really believed it, you could see the horse.

Cowboys and Indians tended to be a game for boys only; girls were not encouraged to join in. One girl asked her grandfather for a cowboy outfit when he took her Christmas shopping and was told 'girls can't be cowboys'.

The excitement of Santa at Christmas for children was as strong in the less commercialised 1950s as it is now. For Dublin and country children alike, a visit to Santa's grotto in Cleary's Department Store on O'Connell Street was a highlight of the Christmas build-up: 'Your heart was always thumping hard by the time you got to stand by Santa's knee.' Parents would buy a blue or a pink ticket; the colour denoted how much was paid for it and the value of the present received from Santa. Presents included jigsaw puzzles, a Mickey Mouse toy, and even a musical instrument known as a Jew's harp that was placed in the mouth and 'could knock your teeth out'.

Other presents given out by Santa to good boys and girls included a package of multi-coloured A4 carbon paper. A sheet was inserted between two ordinary white bits of paper and when one wrote on the top bit, the bottom bit came out red, blue, green, or whatever colour one had used. Cut-out paper dolls on which cut-out paper dresses could be attached were also popular. On Christmas Eve, stockings would be hung up beside the fireplace or at the bottom of the bed, and in the morning, children would excitedly examine the gifts Santa had brought. These were usually very simple presents – crayons and a little colouring book, toy bricks or maybe a Dinky car, a small bar of chocolate, a doll or a teddy bear, or perhaps a book or an annual.

Sport was part of the curriculum in most schools, but for many children, ball games (Gaelic football, soccer or rugby) and other games were part of play as well. At break time, pupils would form makeshift hurling teams or kick a ball around. The GAA's competition for primary schools – Cumann na mBunscol – provided many children with a chance to train and play hurling and football. For girls, there was camogie.

Attending local matches, following one's local parish team or county brought excitement and pleasure into children's lives. The highlight of the year was travelling up to Dublin for the hurling and football finals packed into a lorry or bus or by train. Soccer and rugby were popular in places such as Dublin, Limerick, Athlone, Dundalk and Cork. FAI (Football Association of Ireland) teams such as Bohemians, Shamrock Rovers and Athlone Town had an enthusiastic following among youngsters. Television soccer coverage was still in the future, but many children were fans of English teams such as Manchester United.

Future Taoiseach Bertie Aherne, growing up in North Dublin, has strong memories of the funeral of local boy Liam Whelan, one of the 'Busby Babes' killed in the Munich air crash in 1958. The 'Babes' had played in Dublin only four months earlier. Pupils from Whelan's old school formed a Guard of Honour as the funeral cortege passed by. There were also many children among the Irish fans who attended the controversial Ireland versus Yugoslavia match played at Dalymount Park in 1955.

Youth organisations helped to organise sports events for children. In Dublin and many other towns and cities there were boys' clubs, run by clergy and Gardaí, in which boys got the opportunity to take part in sports such as Gaelic football, soccer, rugby, boxing and running, as well as games such as chess. The clubs organised road races and football matches, with members working off their youthful energy and high spirits doing 3 or 5 mile runs, or working out in the boxing ring. Boxing was a particularly popular sport, and championship matches were organised between clubs from different towns or schools.

In 1950, the *Irish Press* reported on the De La Salle Boys' Club in Wicklow. The club had been set up by the De La Salle Brothers, who ran a local school:

A long narrow hall full of boys and the resounding noise that only boys can produce, billiards, thudding feet at table tennis, boys bouncing rings on boards, boys chatting and laughing, boys huddled in earnest thought over chess and draughts or dominoes, playing cards, reading.

The report explained that the club, based in a hall, was 'run by boys for boys'. The hall was open from 9 a.m. to 9 p.m., and was for both primary and secondary school boys. The club charged an annual fee of 2/6*d*. The club was specially used for boys who cycled long distances, giving them a place to relax after lunch. After school, the town boys came back to play and read. Once a week, one of the De La Salle Brothers gave chess lessons. The boys ran the club through a committee elected annually. The chair of the committee that year was 15-year-old

Sean Fallon who was in the school on a county council scholarship. He explained the rules of the club and how discipline was enforced: 'If you don't behave yourself you get chucked out and that's all there is to it.'

Bray's Our Lady's Boys Club opened on 15 August 1950, following major fundraising efforts by local adults, including a dance on the opening night in the 4,000 sq. ft hall, which was attended by 1,100 people. Archbishop McQuaid of Dublin encouraged the setting up of youth clubs to keep children and teenagers out of harm. In 1957, the Oliver Plunkett Club in Drogheda was praised by a priest as 'a powerful antidote to juvenile delinquency'. In 1956, Cabra Boys' Club in Dublin hosted a visit by pupils from Pudsey Grammar School in Yorkshire. By 1955, there were fourteen St John Bosco Boys' Clubs in Dublin alone.

Children were also taken climbing or taught to swim. A newspaper reported on a school sports day, noting the 'zest' with which the children took part in the three-legged race, the egg and spoon race and the sack race. In Wicklow, a number of boys put together a raft and went rafting on the Liffey River.

Other youth organisations such as the Catholic Boy Scouts of Ireland and the Boys' Brigade also gave members the chance to play sport. The Boys' Brigade offered rugby and gym while the Scouts favoured Gaelic games. Sports for girls were less varied than for boys. Camogie was the most popular in country areas. Hockey and tennis were taught in many convent schools, and Ireland's women's hockey team attracted an enthusiastic following of teenage girls to their international matches. Street hockey was also played. A lot of girls joined tennis, badminton and swimming clubs.

In a number of towns, street leagues were organised to take part in Gaelic football or soccer competitions for children. The leagues were popular and were fiercely competitive, with boys eager to uphold the glory and honour of their street. With every house on the street having an average of four or five children, there was never a lack of players for the leagues:

> With ceremony befitting a great occasion, the final of the Street League took place in Ballinrobe on Wednesday evening. The band was out, and cheering, flag-waving young enthusiasts paraded from the CBS to the playing pitch.

One Westmeath man remembered getting a present of football boots from his father, who was working in England: 'As there was no TV I had to imagine what the game was like.' Some of his friends had got a new leather ball, and they started 'kicking it to one another – they didn't bother to pick it up but kept it on the ground'. One player had a team shirt of 'black and amber with hoops – the first time I had seen the kit of Wolverhampton Wanderers'.

Cricket was also played in some places, with home-made bats and phrases picked up from comics such as the *Hotspur*. On summer evenings, shouts of 'LBW!' 'Six!' or 'Over!' would resound in the air of Irish streets.

Pupils from Presentation Junior School, Mullingar, Co. Westmeath, with their teacher, *c.* 1958. (Mullingar Cathedral Archives)

Pupils from C.B.S. Mullingar, Co. Westmeath, celebrating the School Centenary, June 1956. (Mullingar Cathedral Archives)

Pupils and staff at the opening of the Primary School, C.B.S. Mullingar, Co. Westmeath, October 1959. (Mullingar St Mary's College Archive)

Pupils of The Bower School, Athlone, Co. Westmeath, enjoying the school's sports facilities, *c*. 1950. (Westmeath County Library)

Athlone children from Summerhill orphanage on an excursion to Galway, *c*. 1955. (*Westmeath Independent*)

Children from Co. Westmeath on a school outing to Dublin Zoo, 1954.
(Tom Bell, Castletown-Geoghegan History)

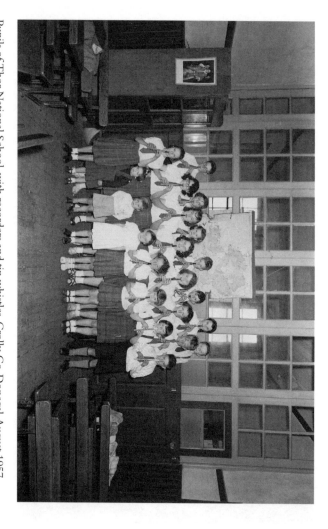

Pupils of Thor National School, with recorders and tin whistles, Crolly, Co. Donegal, August 1957. (National Library of Ireland, Tynan Collection)

Children's Marching Band at the Tidy Towns Plaque unveiling, Glenties, Co. Donegal, *c.* 1959. (National Library of Ireland, Tynan Collection)

Girls in their communion dresses walking from a shrine in Letterkenny, Co. Donegal, *c.* 1957. (National Library of Ireland, Tynan Collection)

Group of boys in their communion suits holding their rosary beads, Co. Donegal, c. 1957. (National Library of Ireland, Tynan Collection)

Pupils of Presentation School, Mullingar, Co. Westmeath, celebrating the Marian Year in 1954. (Meath Diocesan Archives)

Children enjoying a visit to Santa and a spin on the Showboat in Cork, December 1957. (*Cork Examiner*)

A crowd watching boys go-kart racing, Co. Donegal, *c.* 1959.
(National Library of Ireland, Tynan Collection)

A crowd of children following a circus elephant in Mullingar,
Co. Westmeath, *c.* 1959. (Westmeath County Library Archive)

Two boys and a caravan at the O'Brien–Sheridan Traveller Camp, Lough Rea, Co. Galway, May 1954. (National Library of Ireland, Wiltshire Collection)

A group of children stand outside Smith's Pub, Ringsend, Dublin, 16 June 1954. (National Library of Ireland, Wiltshire Collection)

Children looking at the aftermath of severe floods in Athlone, Co. Westmeath, December 1954.
(*Westmeath Independent*)

5

Comics, Cinemas and Circuses

For the children of 1950s Ireland, the highlight of the week was getting their hands on their favourite comics. The 1950s were something of a golden age for children's comics, and there were a wide variety of titles for boys and girls, mostly English, including *The Dandy*, *The Beano*, *Topper*, *Bunty* and *Hotspur*. There was also an Irish comic called *Our Boys*. The comics usually came out weekly on Wednesdays or Thursdays. One man remembered how, 'Thursday evening was the big one in our house in the mid 1950s. "The Comics" were delivered to the local shop.' When his mother came home from shopping she would have *The Beano* and *The Dandy* in her bag.

The comics heralded the coming of the weekend. They would be read over and over throughout the weekend and discussed on the way to school on Monday morning. Comics were passed around among school friends and handed down to younger siblings. Another man recalled some of his happiest memories were of '*The Dandy* and other comics arriving into the local newsagents – precious cargo every Wednesday'. Everyone had their favourite characters in *The Beano* and *The Dandy* – the Bash Street Kids, Lord Snooty, Minnie the Minx, Desperate Dan and his cow pies, Dennis the Menace and his dog Gnasher, Roger the Dodger, Bird the Bear, Little Plum – Your Redskin Chum and Beryl the Peril. Comics such as *Hotspur* and *Victor* were also much read, with their stories of fighting 'The Jerries' in two world wars, and cowboy and Indian Western adventures. *The Eagle*, with its hero Dan Dare – Space Pilot of the Future, was also popular.

For girls, comics included *Bunty* and *School Friend*, with their stories of boarding school chums and midnight feasts, and of orphan girls overcoming enormous odds. One story, *The Four Marys*, about four boarding school friends all called Mary (Mary Radleigh, Mary Simms, Mary Cottor and Mary Field), was particularly popular because there were so many girls called Mary in Irish schools.

Science fiction, Western and horror comics from America such as *Frankenstein* and *Godzilla* were popular with a lot of teenagers, but there was a moral panic around 1955 about horror comic books, and the government was urged to take steps to ban such imports.

There was one major Irish comic in the fifties, *Our Boys*, which was produced by the Christian Brothers. It was similar to the *Victor* and other English comics in

that it featured adventure, detective, war and school stories. However, *Our Boys* substituted Irish nationalism for
the 'England is Best' outlook of the English comics. In
Our Boys, the heroes were historical characters such as
Robert Emmet or Patrick Pearse, and the battles were
set during the 1798 or 1916 rebellions, with the English
occupying the role of villains, which the Germans and
Japanese held in the English comics. *Our Boys* also had a
strong religious ethos in which the heroes were devout
and always said their prayers. The comic was also written
in both English and Irish. There was a version for girls
as well, but it was never as successful as the one for boys.
Our Boys was popular enough, but was never in serious
competition with the English comics.

In a pre-television age, many children spent a lot of
their leisure time reading. Picture books were often
among the first presents given to infants. Some children
were lucky enough to attend primary schools where
there were libraries. In such schools, pupils were usually
able to borrow books on a Friday, with the books kept
in the teacher's room or desk. There were teachers who
made use of the curriculum-free hour they were allowed
once a week to read stories to the pupils. Library services were improving across the country, and thousands
of children were enrolled in county libraries from ages
6 and 7 onwards.

In the library, children could immerse themselves in
worlds of school, war and adventure stories and receive
an introduction to books such as *Huckleberry Finn*, *Anne*

of Green Gables, *Treasure Island*, *Little Women* and many others. A Midlands woman recalled her local 'well-stocked library', where she read *Little Women*, *What Katy Did*, and other classics. A woman who grew up in the Liberties neighbourhood of Dublin described how, 'On a wet day, we had the shelter of Thomas Street library, our gateway to a world of make-believe in the company of Biggles' wartime heroes and Blyton's *Famous Five* adventures.'

Favourite children's authors included Enid Blyton, Angela Brazil, and Richmal Crompton. Blyton's *Famous Five*, *Secret Seven*, *Mallory Towers* and *Noddy* books were great favourites. One Midlands woman recalled how she really looked forward to going to boarding school after completing the *Mallory Towers* school stories. Angela Brazil's boarding school stories and the *Chalet School* books set in a boarding school in Switzerland, were popular with girls, and Richmal Crompton's *William* books about the irrepressible 11-year-old William Brown appealed to both boys and girls. The *Billy Bunter* stories by Frank Richards, first published in 1908, were still popular in the fifties and gained a new audience when they began to appear in book form towards the end of the decade.

Cinema was one of the most important forms of entertainment in mid-twentieth-century Ireland. There were ten cinemas in the O'Connell Street area of Dublin alone, and every provincial town had at least one, some-times two. While extreme nationalists bemoaned the 'Hollywoodisation' of Ireland and the threat to native cul-ture, adults and children alike flocked to see the latest films

from America and Britain and were enormously excited
when screen stars such as John Wayne and Maureen O'Hara,
Bing Crosby and Grace Kelly came to Ireland.

For children, the Saturday morning or Sunday afternoon matinee was a highlight of the weekend. The
matinees included cartoons and cowboy films; one
Dublin cinema was popularly known as The Ranch
because it showed mainly Westerns. Matinee tickets
were 4p (the 'fourpenny rush'), and children could buy
a selection of sweets for another couple of pence – bulls
eyes, Cleeves toffees or gobstoppers to suck or chew on
during the film. Action movies included *Flash Gordon*,
while the cowboy films included *The Lone Ranger* and
Hopalong Cassidy.

The matinees could be completely anarchic occasions,
with children packed into the cinemas shouting, singing, fighting and pushing. At the Bohemian cinema in
Phibsborough – popularly known as 'The Boh' – the
hard-to-control kids were 'regularly flung out by the
hard-pressed ushers'. A teenager described her local
cinema during a matinee as being full of 'seething masses
of small fry, fighting, jumping, wrestling, standing on
their heads, walking on their hands and eating – everybody was eating'.

Westerns and cartoons were popularly known as
'Follyer-uppers'. They were so-called because, as one
Dubliner who spent many a Sunday afternoon at the
matinee in Teranure's Classic Cinema explained, 'The
film was often a follow-on from the week before, where

the hero miraculously survives for another film.' A typical cinema experience for children and teenagers at a major Dublin cinema such as the Savoy or the Theatre Royal – which could seat up to 4,000 in the auditorium – included a Laurel and Hardy or Charlie Chaplin film, a cowboy film, and live variety acts and orchestras. In 1956, teenagers flocked to cinemas to see *Rock Around the Clock* and dance in the aisles. In an era of black and white televisions, the cinema offered children perhaps their first chance to see vivid colour on screen. Author Deirdre Purcell remembers seeing *The Robe* in her local cinema in Dublin in 1953 and being: 'knocked for six by the decibels booming in my ears and the vividness of the colour'.

In country areas, where there were no cinemas, films were often shown in local halls. It was a 'great treat' for country children to be able to go to cinemas such as the Longford Odeon, and 'to marvel at the films coming all the way from Hollywood'.

The circus was another great source of entertainment for Irish children in the 1950s. Circuses such as Duffy's toured the country, setting up camp on fair greens or other open spaces and giving children and adults alike the thrill of seeing a variety of exotic wildlife, as well as clowns and trapeze artists. When the Great Chipperfield Circus came to Dublin in 1956, thousands of children lined the city centre streets to watch the procession of elephants, horses, llamas and other animals go by. The shows were packed out with excited youngsters, including 500 orphans who were brought along as a special treat, and many of them were able to get up very close to the animals indeed. One girl was even carried around by an elephant's trunk! There were lions and tigers, horses and chimpanzees, as well as all the human entertainers, including fire-eaters and girls dancing on horses. Health and safety does not appear to have worried the authorities too much. In country towns, the circus elephants were often paraded across streets, with excited boys and girls walking alongside, underneath and in front of the great beasts.

The zoo was another enjoyable day out for children, whether they were taken by school or parents. At Dublin Zoo, one could get a ride on an elephant or watch a chimpanzee tea party. The crocodiles caused terror and amazement in equal amounts as they opened their enormous jaws filled with sharp teeth.

The Christmas pantomime at the Gaiety Theatre was a highlight of the year for many children in Dublin. The stars of the pantomime included Maureen Potter, Jimmy O'Dea and Milo O'Shea, and the glamorous dancers known as the Royalettes high-kicked their way across the stage. The pantomimes were a special treat for children from orphanages and industrial schools, who were brought to the shows by the Lord Mayor of Dublin. The broadcaster Kevin Hough remembered the thrill of 'going to the panto and there'd be the sweets and the chocolates and the spectacle of *Snow White and the Seven Dwarfs*. They had a revolve on the stage – imagine a revolve in Dublin.'

Irish traditional music and dance events were another place of entertainment, with many children taking part in competitions. The All-Ireland Fleadhs began in 1951 under the auspices of Comhaltas Ceoltóirí Éireann, and traditional gatherings known as *Aeriochta* were still popular in rural districts into the 1950s. As mentioned earlier, many children took part in or watched the major cultural pageants known as *An Tostál*, which were held in the mid 1950s, and which involved theatre productions, choirs and dance all across the country. The Gael Linn Championships in Traditional Irish Song, Dance and Recitation also attracted large numbers of children and teenagers.

Television began in Ireland in the early 1950s with the opening of BBC transmitters in Northern Ireland in 1953, which could be picked up in border regions, and then the opening of ITV in 1955, which could be picked up along the east coast. Ulster Television opened its service in 1959. By 1955, there were 4,000 television sets in Ireland and this had increased to 20,000 by 1958. Those children with access to the black and white, frequently snowy, TV broadcasts of the day could watch children's programmes such as *Watch with Mother*, *The Woodentops*, *Muffin the Mule* and *Andy Pandy*. Some children got to watch the coronation of Queen Elizabeth in 1953 and the wedding of the decade – that of Grace Kelly to Prince Rainier of Monaco in 1956.

Radio stations such as the National Broadcaster, Radio Eireann and the BBC provided a number of children's

programmes. Older children and teenagers could listen
to shows such as *The Kennedys of Castleross* (a soap opera),
Ciaran McMhathuna's request show, the Irish Hospitals'
Sweepstake programme, and even a programme called
The Waltons with its catchphrase 'if you feel like singing, do sing an Irish song', to which the audience could
dance along. The singer Joe Dolan remembered listening
to these dance programmes, 'where you could hear the
feet thumping on the floor'.

In some households, children joined their parents in
performing music around the kitchen table. Joe Dolan,
for example, was taught many Irish traditional songs
by his music-loving mother. Paddy Crosby's *The School
Around the Corner* programme went around the schools
recording children reciting poetry, singing and answering
quiz questions. Broadcaster Kevin Haugh recalls listening
to the Sunday play on Radio Eireann: 'If it was a thriller,
you would be afraid to go to bed that night.'

For many teenagers, however, the radio station of
choice was Radio Luxembourg, which broadcast pop
music programmes such as *Smash Hits* and the top
twenty chart hits. For so many, Radio Luxembourg was
where they first heard the music of Elvis Presley, Buddy
Holly, Cliff Richard and the other early stars of the rock
and roll era. As one Connemara man remembered, 'Rock
'n' roll was coming out – the Radio Luxembourg top
twenty every Sunday night. Usually it was Elvis Presley,
and it was dynamite, just the sound of it would get
you going.'

Irish teenagers – like their British, American and continental counterparts – devoured new music, read new magazines aimed at teens, and bought records. New technologies such as the LP, which came out in 1952, and portable radios, offered new entertainment for Irish teenagers, as did a new home-grown phenomenon: showbands such as the Clipper Charlton, whose era began in dance halls up and down the country from the middle of the 1950s. One particularly popular form of music was skiffle. In households and halls across Ireland, teenagers gathered to make a very basic form of music using washboards as their main instrument.

In the 1950s, a family holiday could mean a week or a fortnight visiting relatives 'down the country' – playing in fields with country cousins. Savings clubs in businesses enabled parents to take their offspring to Butlin's Holiday Camp at Mosney, where organised games were available for children and there were lots of facilities for playing sports such as tennis, football or swimming, while Mum and Dad relaxed. Sports and entertainment for children were also offered by organisations such as the Scouts and Guides associations, the Boys' Brigade, and – for teenagers – the An Óige hostelling movement, as well as the aforementioned Boys' Clubs.

Thousands of children were enrolled as Boy Scouts or Girl Guides (Brownies). In 1950, a new home for Girl Guides was opened in Powerscourt, and in 1959, Lady Baden-Powell visited Ireland and met hundreds of Girl Guides at a rally in the National Boxing Arena, where the programme included singing and dancing. The Irish edition of the Girl Guide movement handbook included badges for Irish dancing and use of the Irish language. Around 3,500 Irish Guides took part in a huge jamboree held in 1957 to mark the Golden Jubilee of the Scouting movement.

For children in a number of places, there was also an opportunity to attend ballet, Irish dancing or art classes. One woman criss-crossed the country, giving ballet lessons in western and Midlands towns. A lot of towns had marching bands, which children and teenagers could join.

Children in the 1950s were resourceful and imaginative, well capable of entertaining themselves in a myriad of ways, with simple toys or no toys at all. They were given a freedom to explore the world around them and enjoy themselves by parents that, perhaps, few children get today, while also having the chance to be entertained at the cinema, the pantomime and the sports ground.

6

Religion

Ireland in the 1950s was a deeply religious country, in which weekly Mass attendance among the Roman Catholic majority was as high as 90 per cent and the year was punctuated by religious festivals, holy days and processions. Children of all faith traditions grew up in a world of religious observance and of strong deference towards clergy.

For most children, religious practice began in the home, where there were often pictures of the Sacred Heart or the Child of Prague or other holy relics and pictures on the mantelpiece or the dresser. The Child of Prague was a particular object of devotion as it was believed to bring good luck. Children were told to pray to St Anthony, patron saint of lost objects, if they lost toys or anything else. Another popular saint was St Jude, who is a patron saint of lost causes.

Across Ireland, before going to bed, children would join in the saying of a decade or two of the rosary. The family would kneel beside a table or chairs while the parents – usually the mother – led the prayers. The children made the responses and the older ones were often asked to say one of the Hail Marys. Some families were particularly devout, saying more than one decade of the rosary and adding in other prayers as well. Alice Taylor has written about how her mother would add numerous additional prayers to the evening rosary recitation: 'First came the litany, starting "Holy Mary", and we would say "Pray for us" in response, after "Holy Mary". There were three Hail Marys for this neighbour and three Hail Marys for another.'

One woman remembered how she and her siblings would try and escape the nightly prayers, but would be ordered down from their room: 'We counted legs of chairs and spoons and turf when our decades came along. We pinched each other and put out our tongues at one another and then took a fit of laughing.'

The nightly rosary might also be followed by prayers before getting into bed and going to sleep, prayers said before and after meals in many a household as well. In Catholic homes, children learned to pray to an impressive array of saints, including Brigid, Patrick, Anthony, Philomena and Agnes:

There was always a feeling of God around and this all came from our parents and neighbours. Everyone was always blessed with holy water leaving a house. Holy water was put on sick cows and St Martin's medal put on everything.

The main purpose of primary school was to train children to fear and love God, and to assist parents in the religious upbringing of their children. Prayers were said at the start of the school day (and in secondary schools, often at the start of each class). Religious Education was a part of the daily curriculum, and also took place in church on Sunday after Mass, when the priest would give half an hour or so of religious instruction.

For Protestant children, Sunday normally meant Sunday School, with children leaving the Service at some point to go into another room for instruction, or attending school before or after Service, where they learned about Jesus and read Bible stories or drew religious pictures. For Catholic children, the first major rite of passage in their religious lives was First Holy Communion, which generally took place at the age of 7 or 8, when the child was in first or second class. The year leading up to the First Communion ceremony – which then, as now, normally took place in May – saw intensive preparations, with large amounts of time in and outside the classroom spent learning about the significance of the sacrament and the importance of prayer.

First Holy Communion was preceded by a child's First Confession, and this, too, was a big occasion. The religion of the 1950s was often a bleak affair, in which children were taught about sin, hellfire and damnation, and learned that this earthly life was nothing much more than 'a vale of tears'. Writer Desmond Ellis remembered how the priest preparing his class for Communion would tell them about 'the extreme and eternal agony of the fiery furnace of hell'. The teachers and priests prepared the child, who would already have been taught the concept of original sin, on how to confess their sins properly, or, as it was termed, to make a 'good confession'. On the big day, the children would troop into church and await their turn to enter the dark confession box and confess to such sins as 'not doing what they were told by their parents' or 'kicking their little brother' and similar.

Most teachers and priests were kind to the little ones, but not all of them. In many parishes, there were priests who had a reputation for being 'very cross', and on their visits to confession, children would try to avoid these priests – not always successfully. For the rest of their school days, children would be sent down to confession on Saturday morning, even if they did not have any sins to tell. Confession was considered to be good and important for the eternal soul.

First Communion was a big day in the lives of 1950s Catholic children, with perhaps a greater sense of its religious meaning and significance than would be the case in the present century. Like their parents, children fasted from midnight on the eve of Communion. They often worried about what would happen if they accidently swallowed a fly or something else during those hours of fasting, and whether they could drink water. It was quite common for children to faint from hunger in the church: 'All that happened was that you were dragged out and given water from the cruets. If you fainted after Holy Communion or got sick, this was another story. The priest had to be told, and he came down after mass and washed the ground around.'

At the First Communion ceremony, the girls wore veils and boys usually had a new shirt and a tie. Elaborate meals and other celebrations to mark the occasion did not usually take place. Instead, the child might be taken out for ice cream or given money to buy sweets: 'Nobody had much money. What you got from your relations on your Communion day could be spent in a spree on lucky bags.'

For some children in Dublin, the day was celebrated with lunch in Clery's Department Store. One woman remembers how, in her area of the Midlands on First Communion day, 'the best china cup and saucer were rooted out of the glass case at home. After the Communion all the children were brought into the convent for breakfast.'

The next major landmark for children was Confirmation. In some parishes, Confirmation ceremonies were held annually, while in others, they took place once every three years. Again, preparation for the ceremony took place over a period of months. Children generally made their Confirmation between the ages of 11 and 13. Preparation involved close study of scripture and of the Catechism. Confirmation marked the moment when a child was welcomed into the world of adult worship and hours were spent learning answers to Catechism questions such as the differences between venial and mortal sins (missing Mass deliberately was a mortal sin, for example). Desmond Ellis remembered his class being told by a priest that they had 'one soul to save and an eternity in heaven or hell to prepare for'.

Those preparing for Confirmation spent long hours in church after Mass, in addition to the time spent in the classroom. A feature of Confirmation days at that time was the bishop who was confirming the youngsters would ask a number of such questions. This was why it was important to know all the right answers to Catechism questions. Confirmation was not just a rite of passage – it was an exam. Children making Confirmation wore cards on a ribbon around their necks, denoting whether they had passed with distinction when questioned on their theological knowledge, or had just passed. Different colours – blue, red, yellow, white – denoted the different levels of success. Red was for honours, blue for second class honours, yellow a pass. An effort would be made by teachers and Catechist to ensure that only the children who knew the right answers would be put forward to stand before the bishop and answer his questions.

In some schools, children who were considered 'slow', or otherwise incapable of giving the correct responses, were withheld from receiving Confirmation – a deeply humiliating act ('a few children always had to go to the bishop who were not up to scratch on the morning of the Confirmation to be heard by him') – as everyone would know who had passed and who had failed. The questions asked were usually quite simple ones, but there were occasions when a child could be confronted with a question such as 'What is transubstantiation?' or 'What are the two natures of Christ?'

The archaic language used in the Catechisms could confuse children too; one boy thought that there were three rather than two types of sin because the answer in the Catechism to a question about the number of types of sin was: 'There are two types of sin; to wit, mortal and venial.' The boy thought that 'to wit' was a third kind of sin. Teachers acted as sponsors for pupils making Confirmation. One man recalled Confirmation as a ceremony in which 'the Holy Spirit descended on us and we were supposed to be able to speak in tongues – whether we were or not, we never found out'.

A man who grew up in a rural area of the Midlands remembered the year as being shaped by religious feast days and the preparations for those festivals:

After Christmas, we had the long, dark days of Lent with the devotions and fasting, broken only by St Patrick's Day, and then down the hill to Easter, hardly had we Lent and Easter over then we had the May devotions, so all in all we spent a lot of time kneeling and praying, going on retreats, fasting, imploring, beseeching and praying.

The strong religious spirit that permeated school life extended to animals. A former student at a country school recalled how 'any bird that we found dead was brought into the chapel and blessed, and buried under leaves'.

In rural areas, as one woman remembered, 'People would always listen for the Angelus bell ringing out at 12 p.m. and 6 p.m. Everyone stopped what they were doing and said the Angelus. You would hear the ringing for miles.'

There were religious devotions known as the Nine First Fridays (Novenas), which were extremely popular. Those performing it had to go to Mass and receive Holy Communion on the First Friday of nine consecutive months. They also had to spend an hour meditating in the Sacred Heart in front of the Tabernacle. The Feast of the Sacred Heart was located within the Octave of the Feast of Corpus Christi, which took place nine weeks after Easter. Some people, especially the often remarkably devout mothers of the era, would also do thirty or forty days of prayers for what were called 'Special Intentions'. It was believed that Our Lord had promised to 'grant to those who receive Holy Communion nine First Fridays of consecutive months, the grace of final repentance. They will not die under my displeasure or without receiving the sacraments.' This was according to the visions of Margaret Mary Alocoque.

Devotions such as the nine Fridays were very popular with teenage girls in 1950s Ireland. A woman who was working in Dublin at the time and staying in a hostel run by nuns recalls how she and her friends frequently visited churches such as the White Friars in Clarendon Street to pray and meditate: 'There were always girls doing Novenas.'

Many who grew up in the 1950s recall the religious beliefs and practice of the era as being an intensely miserable experience: 'We were filled with guilt and shame, and from such a young age.' An example of this singularly bleak brand of religion – with its emphasis on 'mourning and weeping in this valley of tears' was this prayer to Our Lady, which children learned to recite:

> Mary, Queen of Virgins, Mother of Hope to rejected and desolate souls, cast an eye of pity on this child of Eve and hear my prayer. In just punishment for my sins I find myself encompassed with evils and oppressed with anguish of spirit. Whither can I fly than to thee?

Fear of God, hell and damnation played a central role in much religious teaching of the day, in addition to rote learning of Catechism, which taught children to parrot answers they often barely understood. These are some examples of the questions and answers that were learned from the Maynooth and the Penny Catechisms:

> Who made you?
> Answer: God made me.
> Why did God make you?

Answer: God made me to know him, love him, and serve him in this world, and to be happy with him forever in the next.

What is faith?

Answer: Faith is a supernatural gift of God, which enables us to believe without doubting whatever God has revealed.

Children, who were assumed to have attained the use of reason by the age of 7, were also taught in the Penny Catechism: 'Our natural inclinations are prone to evil from our very childhood, and if not corrected by self-denial, they will certainly carry us to hell.'

Children were also taught to believe in the existence of the Devil. The Catechism defined the Devil as 'Satan and all his wicked angels, who are ever scheming to draw us into sin'.

Catholic children were also taught that the Roman Catholic Church was the one true Church and that only those who belonged to the Church would be saved. Protestant children similarly learned that Catholics were wrong.

When it came to learning about sin, many children were taught about 'purity'. Some boys were taught that men were basically animals and women sources of temptation and even evil, and they were warned against 'impure thoughts'. Girls were often taught about the importance of chastity and purity and pointed towards the Virgin Mary as the ideal role model; teenagers were warned against 'company keeping'. The church in

1950s Ireland was often a very harsh and authoritarian institution with a bleak view of human nature and enormous power over people's lives. Every Lent, bishops would issue what were known as 'Lenten Pastorals', and these pastorals would urge children to be obedient to their parents and teachers and priests, and urge parents to ensure that they brought their children up in reverence and fear of the Lord. Women were urged to have many children – the more children the better.

The rules of the Roman Catholic Church decreed that unbaptised infants could not be buried in consecrated ground. Across the countryside, there were burial places for these unbaptised babies, known as *Cillíní*. The burials would be carried out by men. One woman recalls her father and some other man 'burying a baby or two'. These babies died before being baptised and probably at birth. The burials always took place after dark: 'Holy water was always in houses and everyone said prayers, so there was no big deal about burying children without a priest as the people were very familiar with their own prayers. They led the prayers on those occasions.'

Not all of the religious experiences of 1950s children were bleak ones, however. For a great many children, religion brought colour and excitement into their lives. For some, religion brought consolation in bleak, impoverished lives. For others, it brought a sense of purpose and importance – particularly for those who were altar servers, or who got to march in the great religious processions, which were such a feature of the age.

To be an altar server was an important and prestigious role for a boy. Former altar server George O'Brien has written about how 'being an altar boy was the first experience I had of completeness – the notion that the show couldn't go without me'. Altar boys usually began training for their role when they were 8 or 9 (girls were not allowed to be altar servers at that time). Knowledge of Latin was essential, since the Mass was said in Latin in those pre-Second Vatican Council days. One former altar boy recalled the problems posed by one priest he served who said the Latin phrases at incredible speed and expected the altar servers to be able to do the same: 'He started to recite the next prayer before the unfortunate servers had finished the response to the previous one. This led to considerable deterioration in the Latin pronunciation.'

The altar servers worked hard, often having to be at church before 8 a.m. to get things ready for an early Mass. On Sundays, there could be two or three Masses to be served. There were also, on occasions such as Easter and the Feast of Corpus Christi, very elaborate ceremonies known as 'High Masses', with Benediction and large numbers of prayers. Funerals and weddings were other big occasions, as well as 'Missions', when clergy would visit the parish and preach and say Masses every night for a week or two.

Priests could sometimes be harsh with the altar servers. One priest slapped an altar server on the cheek in front of the whole congregation when the child moved the Mass book at the wrong moment. Another boy was slapped by the same priest for failing to tie some essential knots when helping the priest to robe before Mass. Yet another server was sent during mass to fetch an article from the vestry. Unable to find the object, the altar boy left the church and did not return: 'The rest of the mass was punctuated with the priest yelling to the absent boy to "come out here", in between saying the Latin prayers.'

Some boys were particularly devout and their years as altar servers – which generally ended when they were about 12 or 13 – was the first step on the road to priesthood. Others enjoyed the sense of importance of playing a vital role in the saying of the Mass, and of listening to priests lashing the congregation before them for their manifold sins and wickedness, while they sat on the sanctuary altar steps beside or behind the priest, gazing out at the sinners. There were also certain bonuses to the job to make up for the hard work. The boys sometimes received money from offerings given at funerals or other Masses, and had breakfast served to them along with the priest.

Missions were a major part of Catholic religious life in the 1950s. The missions were usually given by members of orders such as the Carmelites, Passionists or Redemptrists. Masses would be held for men one night and for women the next. In a number of cases, there were special Masses or 'retreats' for children. The missions also attracted traders who set up stalls close to the church to sell miraculous medals, holy pictures, holy water, prayer books and other items. Children and adults alike gathered to examine and buy the merchandise on display.

Statues of the Child of Prague or of the Virgin Mary or the Sacred Heart were particularly popular.

The missions themselves were occasions of pure theatre, which many children found exciting. The missionaries, one man recalled, 'had two styles of delivery, loud and deafening'. Alice Taylor described the missionaries who visited her Co. Cork parish most summers as being 'as exciting as a travelling roadshow – the missioner on the altar provided a one-man entertainment, which was all the more exciting when he strode back and forth shouting; it was high drama and better again when he thumped the altar'. There was also the drama of sitting in a darkened church lit only with candles, listening to the priest talking about hell and the dangers of dance halls.

Children at the missions loved adorning themselves with brown or green scapulars, rosary beads, and other holy objects. As Alice Taylor wrote: 'We adorned ourselves with anything that could be pinned or hung on.' During the missions, children often sat apart from their parents up near the front of the church. Behaviour wasn't always so reverent. Alice Taylor recalled friends sitting up in the church gallery spitting on the balding heads of the men seated below. For some children, though, the mission and the endless ranting about sin from the preachers gave purpose to their lives, as one altar boy, George O'Brien, wrote: 'I for one took pleasure in my guilt because I felt equipped with a stable identity, that of a sinner.' If the endless recitations of the Virgin Mary's many titles – House of God, Tower of Mary, Star of the Sea, Refuge of Sinners, and 'every type of Queen, Mother and Virgin besides' – could get too much for altar servers and other children, there was the drama and colour of Benediction to compensate: 'Benediction had everything, and its diversions took place at exactly the right time too, at the conclusion of the tedious, inaudible, repetitive rosary.'

For many girls, the most important part of the religious year was May, the month dedicated in the Roman Catholic Church to honouring Mary. It was a time of the year when flowers were placed on doorsteps, many altars were decorated, and children took part in processions around church or convent grounds, sometimes carrying a statute of Our Lady. The children sang hymns such as 'Queen of the May':

> Bring flowers of the rarest
> Bring blossoms the fairest
> From garden and woodland
> And hillside and dale
> Our full hearts are swelling
> Our glad voices telling
> The praise of the loveliest flower of the May
>
> O Mary, we crown thee with blossoms today
> Queen of the Angels and Queen of the May

Some girls were given the job of actually placing a crown of flowers on the head of a statue of Mary. A retired

teacher in Co. Longford remembered her pupils waiting for her 'outside the school door, laden down with
bluebells, primroses, cowslips, daisies and lilac, all set to
decorate the May altar and all the window sills as well'.
May processions gave girls an opportunity to wear their
First Communion dresses and veils, and they scattered
flowers along the path as they walked.

The Corpus Christi processions, which took place
after Trinity Sunday, were another major occasion in the
religious calendar in which children played a major part.
The procession would usually move through the centres
of towns, with the Blessed Sacrament carried beneath
a canopy and often escorted by soldiers or Gardaí. All
the local schools took part in the procession and, again,
children usually wore their Communion outfits or
Confirmation clothes. The girls scattered flowers as they
marched along, supervised by nuns. Hymns were sung,
and those watching on the pavements would sometimes
kneel and pray as the procession passed. Children helped
to put up bunting and flags (usually the Papal flag) and
altars for the occasion.

The procession usually ended with Mass and
Benediction. The journalist Declan Hassett, writing
about the enormous Corpus Christi processions in Cork,
described the bands playing hymns such as 'Faith of Our
Fathers', and the streets and shop windows crowded with
spectators. Hassett acknowledged that there was an air of
triumphalism about the occasion but also remembered it
'as one of the few days when the streets were given over

to the people'. For a young teenager it felt good 'to be with Dad and older brothers and to be part of an adult world. The smartly outfitted honour guard, complete with raised swords, would add to the pomp and circumstance of the occasion.'

Easter ceremonies, more elaborate in Catholic Churches before Vatican II than now, were another big and colourful occasion, with more processions and prayers. Children over 7 who had observed the strictures of Lent could now look forward to eating Easter eggs or other sweets again after forty days of self-denial. In Dublin on Holy Thursday, there was a custom, observed by children as well as adults, of visiting a number of churches (usually seven), to pray. Some recalled that the visits to different churches were not just religious: 'It was sort of an outing and there was a competitive element – we went around comparing altars and flowers and so on – no formal prayers. We genuflected and spent a few minutes adoring the Blessed Sacrament.'

Christmas was a special time of the year, not just because of the receiving of presents, but because it was a deeply spiritual occasion. In rural areas, particularly, there was, as remembered by many children of the era, a magic to Christmas Eve and Christmas Day. On Christmas Eve, a candle would be lit in every household and placed in the window. The whole family would go to Midnight Mass – often walking or travelling in a pony and trap. The crib was an object of awe and reverence. Children were often sprinkled with holy water by their mothers. Orphans in one Dublin convent were allowed to attend

Midnight Mass and were entertained on Christmas Day by a showband playing popular songs of the days such as 'She Wore Red Feathers'.

There were many other holy days throughout the year. In many parts of the country, St Brigid's Day, on 1 February, was still a special day in the 1950s, as it had been for centuries. Crosses of straw and rush or a doll known as a *Brideóg* were made – sometimes by children – and carried from house to house and placed on walls to bring good luck. Pilgrimages were made to 'holy wells' dedicated to the most beloved of Irish saints. Brigid was a popular name for girls in the 1950s, as were other saints' names such as Agnes, Philomena, Theresa and of course, Mary, as well as variations such as Marian, Marie and Máire.

In rural areas, Stations were a major event. The Stations involved Mass being said in a particular house in each parish once a year. The children of the house would be involved with the weeks of preparation for the event – cleaning, polishing, painting and sweeping. To host the Stations was the biggest honour a household could hope for. The children would be bathed the night before and attired in their Sunday best clothes before helping to welcome the visiting priest, who would say Mass in the house and hear confessions. The writer Alice Taylor, whose family once hosted the Stations, remembered being amused at the experience of going to Confession in her own sitting room. Neighbouring children would come with their parents to the ceremony, and the children of the house would help to serve the meal to the clergy and tidy up after the big day.

Children whose mothers or fathers were employed as sacristans in church helped out with tasks such as cleaning the candlesticks. Flower bags and a bottle of Brasso were used for this job. They also helped to make holly wreaths and holly rings for the church Christmas decorations. In one Midlands parish, the sacristan went around with an ass and cart collecting money from parishioners to buy oats for the priest's horse. The sacristan's donkey was a gift from the local bishop and was known as The Bishop. The children would be told by their father to 'go on out there, yoke up The Bishop and get him ready for the road'.

For Roman Catholic children in 1950s Ireland, Our Lady was a particularly important figure. This was the decade when, across the Catholic world, Marian devotion was at its height. Feast days linked to Our Lady such as 15 August (Feast of the Assumption) and 8 December (Feast of the Immaculate Conception) were holy days of obligation, and, again, involved Masses and the placing of flowers on altars to Mary. In 1950, Pope Pius XII proclaimed the Dogma of Mary's Assumption into Heaven. A pupil at Our Lady's Bower Convent School in Athlone described the enchantment of the occasion, which was broadcast on Radio Éireann:

> We sang the Mass of the Assumption, listening to our Holy Father, The Pope, on our knees, as he proclaimed

the Dogma. Everyone was overwhelmed with joy to hear that Our Holy Father was going to proclaim the Dogma of the Assumption on 1 November. His voice sounded so wonderfully clear and impressive as he pronounced the beautiful words of the Dogma.

Across the country, the Mass of the Assumption was sung in all churches on that day, 1 November 1950, and thousands of children and teenagers took part in the ceremonies. Candles were lit in many homes and schools, and churches and other buildings were decorated with flags and bunting.

The year 1954 was proclaimed as a special 'Marian Year' in honour of Mary and marking the centenary of the Proclamation of the Dogma of the Immaculate Conception. Throughout the Marian year, which began on 8 December 1953, there were numerous events in which children – particularly girls – took part, including special Masses and processions and the unveiling of statues and other artworks. During that summer, the country was visited by the charismatic Irish-American priest Father John Peyton, who preached his 'Rosary Crusade' ('The family that prays together stays together') across the land. Children again played an important part in the crusade, singing in choirs and joining the processions to the venues for Fr Peyton's Masses.

In Mullingar, Co. Westmeath, 100 children from the Presentation Convent School took part in the Mass carrying giant rosary beads. Schools were involved in art and music events to mark the Marian celebrations. In Dublin, for example, the pupils of one Loreto convent school devised an elaborate pageant celebrating scenes from the life of Mary and the life of the Church in the century since the Dogma of the Immaculate Conception had been proclaimed. In Co. Limerick, the children of the Kilmallock Convent Primary School gave what was described as a 'very impressive presentation of a pageant called "The Mysteries of the Rosary" in the People's Hall with a cast of over 100'.

Liturgical festivals held in places across the country in the 1950s attracted entries from numerous school choirs, including Mercy Convent, Longford, Our Lady of Good Counsel, New Ross and Moate Mercy Convent. The following year the choir of Our Lady's Bower Athlone, sang at the monastery of Clonmacnoise at a special ceremony marking the handover of the famous monastic site to the State.

On 3 February, the feast day of St Blaise, patron saint of sore throats, children joined parents in church to have their throats blessed. In Dublin, Adam and Eve's Church on Merchant Quay was one of the most popular venues. Street traders would set up shop along the route, offering 'olive oil or flannel, which they claimed could treat throat infections'.

All Souls' Day on 2 November was another important day in the religious calendar. Alice Taylor has written about how, as a secondary student in a school close to a church, she and her friends were 'roped in to contribute long Latin chants whenever there was a High Mass for the dead. We made an enthusiastic group of mourners in our enjoyment at the thought of the classes we were missing.' On All Souls' Day, Taylor and her friends would go in to the church and say prayers for the souls of the dead: 'Our religious fervour increased as lunch hour extended into school time and we waked souls out of purgatory by the dozen.'

There were many other occasions on which special Masses were held. During the 1956 polio epidemic in Cork, a special day of prayer took place and Bishop Lucey of Cork blessed children at the Holy Trinity Church in the city. There was also an annual children's pilgrimage to the Shrine of Our Lady in Knock, Co. Mayo. A 1955 newspaper report about this pilgrimage stated:

> About 20,000 of the youth of Ireland, representative of practically every school, college and university, gathered at Our Lady's Shrine for the annual children's pilgrimage. The Fourth Mayo Troop and First Galway Troop, Catholic Boy Scouts of Ireland and the Catholic Girl Guides formed a guard of honour as the statute of Our Lady was carried at the head of the procession.

Children and teenagers were encouraged to join religious organisations such as the Legion of Mary, the Pioneer Total Abstinence Association and the Children of Mary. The Children of Mary was a junior version of the Sodalities, to which many women belonged. The Sodalities had a quarter of a million members in 823 branches in 1958. The Children of Mary, wearing blue cloaks and white dresses, were a distinctive part of the religious ceremonies of the age, often sitting in the front row at Mass and leading religious processions. The Legion of Mary, founded in Dublin in 1921, was a very popular organisation in 1950s Ireland. Members met for prayer, visited the sick and the poor, and engaged in evangelising work: children and teenagers were enrolled in what were known as Junior Praesidia. As well as taking part in prayer meetings, they were involved in tasks such as delivering the Legion newspaper.

School children were encouraged to join the Pioneer Total Abstinence Association and to pledge to refrain from drinking alcohol. Not all kept the pledge beyond 18, but for some, that childhood pledge would mark the start of a lifelong abstinence. The Pioneers were one of the largest organisations in Ireland at that time, with more than a quarter of a million members. Boys were often encouraged to follow their fathers and grandfathers into the male equivalent of the Sodalities, which was the Holy Family Confraternity. As with the Sodalities, Confraternity members met for prayer regularly and were expected to receive Communion at least once a month.

The Catholic Boy Scouts and Catholic Girl Guides organisations offered children the opportunity to enjoy scouting activities such as camping, and to learn various skills, within a religious ethos. The Catholic Boy

Scouts of Ireland had been set up in the 1920s to offer a Catholic alternative to the Boy Scout Movement, which in Ireland was seen as a largely Protestant organisation. Catholic Scouts and Guides played a part in religious ceremonies such as Corpus Christi processions and the consecration of bishops.

In school and church, children were taught about the heroic work of Irish missionaries in places such as Africa, Korea and China. Prayers were said for bishops, nuns and priests imprisoned by communists, and also for the conversion of Russia. Pennies were collected for 'the black babies' in Africa. A lot of children came to feel that they personally owned a black baby.

Ecumenism did not really exist in mid-twentieth-century Ireland, and Catholics were told that they must not, under any circumstances, enter Protestant churches. One woman remembered sneaking into a Protestant church one day on her way home from school and being disappointed at how ordinary it seemed. When she told her parents what she had done, she was beaten. Others remembered being told that the local Church of Ireland rector was the Devil. In one Ulster town, teenagers were denounced from the altar for attending a dance in a Protestant hall, while Protestant teenagers were urged to avoid Catholic halls. In parts of Dublin, children would chant sectarian slogans at one another. The Catholics would shout:

Proddy, Proddy, go to hell
Ringing out the Devil's bell.

To which the Protestant kids would retort:

> Catty, Catty, go to Mass,
> Riding on the Devil's ass.

Children were caught up in the ugliest episode of sectarianism in the Republic since Independence – the Fethard-on-Sea boycott in 1957. The boycott of Protestant businesses in the small Wexford town started when a Protestant woman in a 'mixed' marriage left the family home and returned to the north with her children after she came under pressure to have the children brought up as Roman Catholics.

Occasionally, Protestant children would be confronted by Catholic children demanding to know whether they believed in the Virgin Mary – and were sometimes hit if they said they didn't. One Protestant woman remembered Catholic processions as occasions 'where we sharply felt our difference'. It should be emphasised, however, that in many parts of the country, Catholic and Protestant children played together and got on just fine.

The historian Tom Garvin played with Protestant and Jewish boys in South Dublin. They decided that the Jews had it cushy as they only had to pray to God. The Protestants had it harder because they had to believe in Jesus as well, while the Catholics had the hardest time, since they had to pray to Mary as well as to God the Father and Jesus. After this theological debate, 'we lost all interest in the knotty problems of theology, a word we had never heard of, and went back to the far more interesting topic of Tommies and Nazis or Japs or Yanks'. Garvin did note, however, that, 'Protestant kids stopped playing with you when they were 12 years of age, an unexplained and much resented mystery.'

For Protestant children, religion also played a significant part in their lives during the 1950s. The majority of them attended primary and secondary schools in which the Protestant ethos prevailed and the local Church of Ireland bishop was patron. Much school time was given to preparing children for Confirmation and most children attended Sunday School. At Sunday School they learned Scripture and sang hymns. Among the hymns was 'Jesus Loves Me':

> Jesus loves me this I know,
> For the Bible tells me so;
> Little ones to him belong –
> They are weak but he is strong.

> Yes, Jesus loves me,
> Yes, Jesus loves me,
> Yes, Jesus loves me,
> The Bible tells me so.

Children at Sunday School were often awarded prizes for their Scripture knowledge. The prize was usually a Bible or some other worthy spiritual book. The Boys' Brigade and the Girls' Friendly Society, to which many Protestant children belonged, had a strong religious ethos and were connected to the Church of Ireland. One Boys' Brigade member remembered how on Sunday, after Sunday School, 'you went to "Boys" Brigade Bible class and then if you weren't lucky, you'd go to church again that night'. A Protestant equivalent of the Pioneer Association was the Band of Hope, which enrolled a number of children and teenagers. In some parts of Ulster, children belonged to Protestant cultural organisations such as the Orange Order as members of the Junior Orange Order, and took part in the 12 July Parades in Co. Donegal or across the border.

Religion played a major part in the lives of Jewish children as well. While many children attended Christian schools such as Wesley College or the High School, Rathgar, most went to Jewish primary and secondary schools in Dublin. Pupils learned Hebrew at school, observed the major Jewish festivals, and had days off school on the High Holy Days such as Yom Kippur and Rosh Hashanah. Boys in the Jewish primary Zion schools had secular schooling from 9 a.m. to 1 p.m., and from 3 p.m. to 5 p.m., they had religious schooling ('Cheder'). Just as the Catholic children could join the Catholic Boy Scouts and Catholic Girl Guides, so Jewish children could join the Dublin Jewish Scout Troop or the Jewish Girl Guide Troop, where again, a religious ethos prevailed.

Roman Catholic boys and girls were encouraged to have a religious vocation. Priests and nuns were held in high regard, and to have a son or daughter become a priest or nun was considered by most Catholic parents to bring huge honour to the family. Religious vocations were at an all-time high in the 1950s, with All Hallows College in the Dublin archdiocese sending dozens of priests to America alone every year. Junior seminaries such as St Finian's College in the diocese of Meath guided boys as young as 13 towards the priesthood, teaching Latin and Theology. Many orders of nuns recruited and trained teenage girls – known as 'postulants' – for the religious life. Large numbers of girls, in particular, were drawn to the religious life, seeing a career as a nun as being as attractive as one as a teacher or a nurse.

A steady stream of boys entered seminaries such as Maynooth, All Hallows, and Carlow from secondary schools right through the decade. Some teenagers were practically forced into orders such as the Christian Brothers by parents anxious to have one less child to feed and clothe. The Christian and Marist Brothers almost acted as parents to many of these teenagers, providing them with an education that their parents could not afford to give them.

Many children retained their membership of organisations such as the Legion of Mary and the Pioneers well into adulthood, and passed on their strong religious beliefs to their own children.

Religion even permeated the world of sport in those days. At GAA matches, players would go down on one knee to kiss the ring of the bishop before he threw in the ball to start the match. Children at these matches would join in the singing of the stirring anthem 'Faith of Our Fathers', a hymn that commemorated the martyrdom of English Catholics during the sixteenth and seventeenth centuries:

Faith of our fathers living still,
In spite of dungeon, fire and sword,
Oh, how our hearts beat high with joy,
Whene'er we hear that glorious word.

Faith of our fathers, holy faith,
We will be true to thee till death.

Many GAA clubs were coached by priests, and the clergy were involved in setting up sports clubs for children and teenagers, acting as religious as well as sporting mentors.

Probably at no time in the twentieth century was Ireland as strongly and intensely a religious – and Catholic – country as it was in the 1950s. For many children, the religious culture of the time was a painful experience, which would lead them to reject the Church when they reached adulthood. For others it was a happy, even joyful, time in their lives, which they would remember with fondness and respect.

7

The World of Work

Irish children in the 1950s often worked very hard. They were often expected to do chores around the house and in school. In large families, the older ones helped to care for younger siblings. Children on farms were expected to help out on the land at harvest time and other occasions, and, for more than half the children of the era, paid employment in the workforce or apprenticeship for a career began when they were still legally considered children, aged 14 or 15. Many of the teenagers who went to work played a vital role in keeping their family financially secure, and often helped keep younger brothers and sisters in education.

For children brought up on farms, the world of work began early. Many boys and girls, before setting out on the often long trek to school, would milk cows, move animals out to pasture, clean out grates and light fires.

After a long day in the classroom, there would be more jobs to be done when they came home – bringing in the livestock from the fields, for example. A teacher in one secondary school admired her hard-working students who, when they returned home, would have to work for two or more hours around the farm before settling down to do their homework.

School attendance inspectors were strict in enforcing attendance and took action against parents who persistently did not ensure that their children were at school. But in country areas, there was a general understanding that at certain times of the year, children would and could absent themselves to help out with vital work such as harvesting and turf cutting and gathering. The threshing was a major day in the agricultural calendar and children joined the *meithil*, or co-operative effort to thresh the grain. While it was adult men who did the threshing, children helped to bring food and drink out to the workers and to tidy up afterwards. The experience of threshing was often a highlight of a child's year, as was the cutting and saving of the turf. The turf saving was 'a great way to whet the appetite and get a good suntan'.

Bringing animals to the market was another job done by youngsters. One Longford man recalled how he helped out with cattle dealing from the age of 12:

Early in the morning I had to drive cattle into Longford station for the Dublin market. My mother would give me the £6 to pay at the station – with the aid of a safety pin she would secure the money in my top breast pocket, then she would give me 6p for myself. Out of the 6p, I would get three bars of chocolate – one for myself and one each for two helpers. When I got back from the station I had to get ready for school. My teacher was very kind – although I was often yawning in class she never punished me.

Children also helped out when their parents were selling turkeys, geese, pigs or cattle at the fairs and marts, which were still an important part of the commercial life of Irish country towns in the 1950s. City children were similarly employed in places such as Dublin's Iveagh and Smithfield markets.

In spring, many country children were kept out of school to plant potatoes ('dropping spuds', as it was known). In May, the turf banks were cleaned and the turf cutting began. In summer, children helped to draw the turf home.

At school, children cleaned out grates and lit fires, swept the classrooms, set tables for teachers' lunch, boiled up kettles to make tea or cocoa for the staff, and washed windows. Some were sent out on messages to get food or collect turf or firewood. Those children who grew up 'over the shop' often helped behind the counter after school and during holidays. A tourist visiting a family-run hotel in a small town recalls being booked into the hotel and shown to his room by a self-assured child aged around 8 or 9, who stood on a box behind the counter so that he could actually be seen by people approaching the reception area.

In many places, children worked half-days in mills and other businesses in the year or two leading up to their departure from education at 14. Although there were increasing calls to raise the school-leaving age to 15 (as happened in Britain and Northern Ireland), 14 remained the leaving age right through the decade, and up to 80 per cent of children entered the workforce on or soon after their fourteenth birthday.

The *Irish Press* ran a series of articles between 1949 and 1950 on employment opportunities under the title 'Any jobs going?' The articles, which covered 117 careers in all, provide a fascinating glimpse into the world of work that teenagers entered in early 1950s Ireland, including opportunities provided for youngsters to further their education while learning a trade. Another series of articles entitled 'Careers' ran in the *Irish Independent* in 1956, looking at 120 different trades and careers. The following are some of the jobs covered by the two papers:

Carpenter

At the start of the 1950s, there were 2,000 apprentices, many aged between 13 and 16. The Woodworking Union gave priority to the sons of carpenters. The apprenticeship lasted for six years. In the first year, apprentices were paid 2*d* an hour. This increased year by year, reaching 2/6d in the sixth year. The newly qualified carpenter (who might then still be only 18 or 19), could then expect to start work at a rate of 3/12½d per hour, plus a 6d a day 'tool money' allowance. The teenage apprentice would spend his first months learning the use of tools and joints: 'The correct handling of saws, planes, and chisels, something that takes time to learn.'

Carpentry courses were on the curriculum of many technical schools, and this was seen as supplementing the practical trade training. Apprentices were allowed time off to attend the classes, which were run by day and by night. There was a fee for these classes of £1 for the day classes and 10s for the night courses. As well as practice in using tools, 'special attention is given to theory and the form of geometry and drawing'. Later on, the apprentice got the opportunity to 'take on pieces of work such as the making of doors, windows and different types of frames'. There was a huge demand for places on technical school carpentry courses, with very long waiting lists.

There was an awareness, too, that many of the would-be apprentices had left school with no qualifications and a lack of learning, so for those considered to be 'deficient in general education', there was a special pre-apprenticeship course, which included maths, drawing, woodwork and English, Irish and religious education.

Hairdresser

This was a job mainly aimed at girls. The *Irish Press* article began, 'If you are over 16 and have passed the Leaving Cert and have a flair for "messing about with hair", then your path is clear.' The Leaving Cert requirement only applied to Dublin city and county and in Cork city. In Dublin and Cork there was a four-year apprenticeship, which began with a salary of 10s a week, rising to £2 a week in year four, with a forty-eight-hour working week. Outside Dublin and Cork, trainees were required to pay an 'indoor apprenticeship' fee of £25 for six months of training or £50 for a year, from which 'you may be paid a small weekly sum'.

Waiter or Waitress

This job required a three-year apprenticeship, during which the apprentice went from a starting wage of 19/6d per week to 32/6d per week in year three. In the early 1950s, a school for the training of waiters was set up by the Hotel Federation and the Hotels and Restaurant Association. At this time, a waitress in a Dublin restaurant could expect to earn 41/6d per week, with 10s 'gratitudes'. In Cork city, a waitress could earn 33s per week. Rates were lower in smaller towns, and waiters earned 20s more than waitresses.

Electrician

In the 1950s, this was a trade to which many boys aspired as there was plenty of work available for electricians due to the rural electricificiation scheme and an extensive programme of house building, which was under way in many towns and cities. In 1956, the *Irish Independent* stated:

> Parents should consider what trade their boy is going to take up as soon as he is ready to leave primary school. For those wishing to be an electrician, it is important to get him into a technical school to do a pre-apprenticeship course.

The aspiring electrician served a five-year apprenticeship. This included attendance at special day courses at a technical school, with the apprentice then apprenticed to a firm of engineers or contractors. The apprentices were nominated by employers and unions, with preference shown to the sons of electricians. The apprentice would spend three months of each year at technical school. For the remaining eight months of the year, he would attend a correspondence course at the school. The subjects including turning, drawing, electrical technology, maths and electrical theory; and exams were set by the technical instructors.

When not in the classroom, the apprentice was receiving on-the-job practical training. He was paid 15*s* per week in year one, rising to 50s a week for the final year. The apprentice also had an opportunity, towards the end of his apprenticeship, to sign up for a two-year course with London University, leading to a BSc qualification.

Motor Mechanic

This was a job with prospects for a teenage boy in the 1950s as the number of cars on Irish and British roads increased. The path into the trade started with a junior day course at the local technical school for one or two years, ending with sitting the Inter Cert exams. Subjects taught included mechanical drawing, woodwork and metalwork, English, maths, mechanics and heat or magnetism and electricity.

A three- or four-year apprenticeship could be served, during which the apprentice was expected to attend suitable classes at the local tech school and to study and pass exams for the trade's Group Certificate. The apprenticeship could be terminated if the exam was not passed by the end of the third year. Day classes cost 4/4d per week, with night classes at 2/5d per week.

Dressmaker

The advice offered to girls who 'have just finished school and want to become a dressmaker' was to join classes in needlework and dressmaking provided by vocational education committee schools. There were some Dublin schools where special day classes were run for 'girls wanting to be apprenticed to women's trades', and evening classes in domestic economy (including needlework and dressmaking): 'These classes will give you a good foundation training in needlework and dressmaking.'

Having attended such classes, the student could then get apprenticed to a dressmaker or to a tailoring or dressmaking firm. These apprenticeships generally lasted four years, with a pay scale rising to 63/40*d* in the fourth year.

National Teachers

At the beginning of the 1950s, there were 10,500 lay teachers in the Irish national school system. Although many teachers began their training after doing the Leaving Cert at 17 or 18, it was possible to begin training earlier. Annual competitive exams were held around Easter for boys and girls between the ages of 13 and 15 to enter preparatory colleges. A quarter of places were reserved for youngsters from Gaeltacht areas or Irish-speaking homes. The exam subjects were Irish, English, arithmetic, history, geography, sewing, penmanship and needlework. The exam standard was that of the Primary Cert.

Those who passed the exam spent four years in one of six preparatory colleges and then a further two years in colleges such as St Patrick's Drumcondra, Carysfort, St Mary's Limerick or Coláiste Moibhí, Dublin. The students sat the Inter Cert exam at the end of second year and the Leaving Cert at the end of fourth year. The fees for students stood at £50 per year, though this could be reduced depending on the financial circumstances of parents. There was also a £30 grant available towards the cost of uniforms and travelling expenses.

Girls aspiring to teach were warned that it was not a career for them if they also wished to marry, since married women had to resign from their jobs. It wasn't until 1958 that married women were permitted to teach. One area of teaching where women were encouraged was P.E. According to the *Irish Independent*, 'Any girl who is seeking an occupation that will be exhilarating, absorbing and energetic and will at the same time promote an excellent sense of physical wellbeing, cannot do better than becoming a P.E. teacher.'

Cabinetmaker

This skilled trade was open to those who served a six-year apprenticeship. The aspiring apprentice had to have the Primary School Cert or to have completed at least one year's attendance full-time in technical school. The weekly wage for an apprentice started at 22*s*, rising to 105*s* a week in the final year. For apprentices living within a 3 mile radius of Bolton Street Technical College in Dublin, day classes in cabinet-making on four days a week given by the college had to be attended in their first two years. In years three and four, there were two night classes a week in Bolton Street. The fees for day classes were £1 a year and for the night classes, 10s a year.

Milliner

For girls aged 14 living in Dublin, the way into this profession was an apprenticeship with a millinery house. The apprenticeship was for four years, with a starting wage of 16/4d per week and a forty-hour working week. The working hours and wages were regulated by the Women's Clothing and Millinery Joint Labour Committee, and apprentices could acquire a 'Learner' card. By the end of the apprenticeship, the pay was £2/12s per week.

Telephonist

In the 1950s, few people had telephones, there was no subscriber trunk dialling (STD), and calls usually had to be routed through a telephonist working for the post office. Candidates had to be 18, but required only a seventh-class national school standard of education. During their two-year training, the trainees were referred to as girl probationers.

Air Mechanic

Applicants for this job had to be 16, with a sixth-class national school standard. They had to have attended full-day classes in a technical school for at least one term.

Barman

At a time when there were far more pubs in Ireland than today, this was a career guaranteeing employment. Many youngsters started working lives helping out in the family pub business. For those wanting to enter the trade, the minimum entry age was 16, and a Primary Cert was required. There was a four-year apprenticeship.

Marine Engineer

This was a career in which preference was given to youngsters whose father was an engineer. No particular standard of education was specified. The apprentice could attend a course in engineering for three years and then spend a further two years learning practical skills in a dockyard or engineering works.

Plumber

This was a trade that many youngsters in the 1950s wanted to join. Building schemes in Ireland and in Britain meant that work was plentiful for trained plumbers. The level of interest in the job was reflected in the fact that, at the beginning of the 1950s, there were 150 plumbing apprentices attending Bolton Street College alone, with hundreds more on waiting lists. Many apprentices began their training at the age of 14, the educational standard for new apprentices was the Primary Cert. Trainees could do a two-year day course, with six hours per week in the classroom, followed by a three-year night course for two nights per week. Vocational committees granted scholarships to apprentices annually. Some employers sent their apprentices to technical schools and paid the fees.

Bricklayer

This trade recruited apprentices aged 14 to 16, with 'sons of bricklayers having a prior claim'. The apprenticeship period was six years, with a fee of £30 per year. In year one, the apprentice could earn 7p per hour, rising to 2/6d per hour in the final year. The apprentice could also attend technical school day or evening classes. Some vocational education committees ran two-year full-time day apprentice courses.

Brass Fitter

Youngsters could enter apprenticeships for this trade at 14, starting with a two-year day course in a technical school, learning Irish, English, science, maths, woodwork and mechanical drawing. Apprentices were usually selected from the technical schools, and the apprenticeship lasted seven years, with compulsory attendance at night classes for four of those years. The starting wage paid was 16*s* a week for the first years.

Glass Worker

This was open to boys aged 16 who had the Primary Cert. The apprenticeship lasted four years.

Laundress

This job was open to girls aged 14 and over. The apprenticeship period was four years, with a fee of £3. By their final year, girls could expect to be earning 20*s*/9*d* per week. In an era before washing machines became common, there was quite a high demand for laundress services from businesses and households.

Boilermaker

This trade took in boys aged 16 as apprentices. The apprenticeship was for five years and 'working practices may be supplemented with technical school classes'. Some techs offered evening classes in welding. First-year apprentices earned 26*s* per year, rising to 68*s* in the last year.

Grocer's Assistant

A Primary Cert was needed for this job, which involved a three-year apprenticeship: 'The duties to be performed by the apprentice were entirely a matter for the employer.' Some technical schools ran day classes for trainees in the grocery and provision trade in co-operation with the employers' associations and employees' trade unions. Evening classes could be taken to secure the Department of Education Advanced certificate in retail practice.

Confectioner

This trade was often a family concern and, according to the *Irish Press*, 'preference is given to those with relatives in the trade'. Boys had to be 16 and to have a Primary Cert. No educational qualifications were required for girls. A two-year apprenticeship in the bakery trade had to be served. The working hours for the apprentice were 8 a.m. to 2.30 p.m., and they received free bread. Apprenticeships lasted for four years, with a starting wage for boys of £2/2s/6d per week, increasing to £3/7s/6d in fourth year. Girls started at £1/1s/3d per week, increasing to £2/2s/6d in the final year. Apprentices could get time off work to attend cookery classes in technical school.

Printer

This was a trade that employed large numbers of people in newspaper offices across Ireland in the pre-computer era. By the middle of the 1950s, entry into the printing trade was by way of a seven-year apprenticeship. Boys had to be 15 years old, have spent two years in technical school, and to have secured the technical Junior Certificate. During their apprenticeship, they had to continue attending suitable day or evening classes in their local tech.

Victualling

For this trade, a boy could become a trainee at the age of 14 but was obliged to attend pre-apprenticeship courses at technical school before becoming an apprentice at 16. During the four years of his apprenticeship, continued attendance at day or evening classes was compulsory. The apprentice was paid a wage that started in his first year at £1/16s/1d per week.

Post Office Worker

In 1956, there were 350 boy messengers employed by the Post Office. They worked delivering telegrams and on 'indoor duties of a simple character'. The path to a permanent and pensionable job at the age of 18 within the semi-State company involved boys attending compulsory evening classes at their local technical school and sitting exams in subjects such as Irish, English, arithmetic, geography and grammar.

Draughtsman

According to the *Irish Independent*:

> There is no reason why a boy who may not have gone to secondary school should not ultimately qualify as a draughtsman, if after primary school, he enrols in a local technical school for a day junior technical course for two years.

The apprenticeship period for this career was five years, and attendance at evening classes in suitable subjects was compulsory. The apprentice was paid a starting wage of £1/12s per week.

Civil Servant

While some areas of the Civil Service required job applicants to be over 17 and to have a Leaving Certificate, there were positions open to younger girls and boys. The educational standard for what were called 'writing assistants' was just the Primary Certificate. Some clerical grades were open to those who had passed the Inter Cert and had reached the age of 16. Those applying for clerical positions sat an exam in Irish, English, maths, handwriting, spelling, grammar and Latin or Greek, or a continental language such as French or German. High pass marks were required in Irish. Shorthand typists could also be recruited from among those under 16, with preference given to those who had attended technical schools.

★★★

These are just some of the potential careers that were covered in the article, the full range included many others such as serving in the army and being a cinema usher or usherette, bus driver or conductor, to railway clerk or boiler worker.

However, many school leavers who went to the employment market were too young or uneducated to have any hope of securing such jobs. Far too many began their working lives in low-skilled or unskilled, poorly paid and often dead-end employment. There were other restrictions on their employment opportunities as well: trade unions enforced strict 'closed shop' agreements that excluded those not in the union. In 1950, the *Irish Press* reported the case of a teenager who had been trained as a carpenter while in Borstal school but was unable to get a job because he was not in a union and was not allowed to join a union because he had been in a Borstal. The president of Cork Chamber of Commerce deplored the existence of 'closed trades' and noted that 'no boy who was not an immediate relative of a tradesman would be accepted as an apprentice in most trades'.

Other job opportunities for youngsters were restricted by sectarian or gender discrimination. Catholic employers preferred to hire Catholics and Protestant ones to hire Protestants – for example the Guinness Brewery restricted some of its jobs to Protestants. The exclusion of girls from science and higher maths classes in many vocational and secondary schools, as well as the exclusion of boys from domestic science classes, created a serious impediment to those seeking work. Girls could not get employment in many skilled trades that were reserved for boys and men. Even a career such as the Gardaí was not open to women until the very end of the decade, the first female Gardaí not being recruited until 1959. Businesses also preferred to hire sons and daughters of employees, and would visit schools and ask pupils how many had fathers working for their company.

One common source of employment for boys was as messengers. In an age when few businesses had cars or telephones, the messenger boys performed an important service delivering goods. One former messenger boy in the Midlands recalled his first job, where he was 'paid £2 a week to deliver messages all round the town in all kinds of weather'. He worked a five-and-a-half day week, with a half-day on Thursdays. The busiest day for him was Saturday, when he worked until 10 p.m. Every couple of weeks, he delivered 100lb of grain to the local bishop's house.

Messenger boys were, as Tom Garvin noted in his book *News from a Republic*, 'commonly exploited labour in what was unmistakably a dead-end and short-term job'. A total of 6,000 messenger boys were recorded in the 1951 census. It was one of the largest sources of employment for teenage boys. Many worked forty-five-hour weeks. The *Irish Press* reported in 1950 how some 14-year-old boys were working 'an 11- to 13-hour day without any increased remuneration'. In 1956, the Limerick branch of the Irish Transport and General Workers' Union (ITGWU) complained that 'some employers consider messenger boys to be less than human, some would not even dream of treating animals in the way they treated messenger boys'.

The boys did not always passively accept poor working conditions, however. In 1951, messenger boys in Cork staged a series of strikes demanding higher wages and the free provision of proper protective clothing against wet and cold weather. Up to 150 boys took to the streets in protest, shouting and cheering.

For girls who left school at 14 or 15, shop work and domestic service were the top employment choices. Personal services – waitressing, laundry work, becoming a cook and domestic service – made up the largest sector of teenage female employment. Even into the 1950s, quite a number of middle-class households employed maids. Again, this work was poorly remunerated. In one town, girls working as extras in a film production were paid more for a day's work than they earned in a week in domestic service. Girls often took up domestic work because they felt they had no other choice. Working class girls were the most likely to end up in these sorts of dead-end jobs because they had less opportunity to improve their social mobility through education, as their parents could not afford to keep them at school.

Factories employed many girls under 18 in the 1950s – in fact, it was one of the largest employment sectors for girls. According to the 1951 census, 22,500 women and worked in factories. One woman in a country town recalled her joy when a factory opened in the town just as she was finishing her schooling. She was able to walk to work from home and bring home much-needed income for the household budget. Factories usually had proper light, heat, a canteen and toilet facilities. For those girls who managed to go on to vocational school and do the Group or Inter Cert, jobs as typists/secretaries, clerks and other better remunerated posts could be obtained.

One area in which neither boys nor girls wished to work was farming. Many 14- or 15-year-old boys left home to avoid the drudgery of unpaid or low-paid work on their fathers' farms or as labourers on some other man's farm. Although governments and religious leaders extolled agriculture as the backbone of the nation, few youngsters saw farming as a job they wished to spend their lives doing. Writing in the *Irish Independent* in 1950, Shane Leslie noted that when children expressed their opinions about careers, 'there is a titter' when a boy expressed a wish to be a farmer. Many parents – and especially mothers – in rural areas were determined to see their children get to a town or city, where opportunities were so much better. Many mothers also wanted their daughters to escape from the domestic drudgery they had endured.

Retail offered reasonable opportunity for a good job for some teenagers. In Dublin, shops such as Guineys in Talbot Street and Frawleys in Thomas Street employed teenagers. One woman, who left school on her four-teenth birthday, remembered being sent by her mother to Frawleys to get work. There was no interview – she gave her name and age and was told to report for work on the following Monday. She began her working life selling dolls in the toy department. A teenage boy who applied for a job in the same business was given a piece of paper with the sums 2/11*d*, 4/11*d*, 9/11*d* and 1/1*d* written on it, and told to add up the figures. Having done so correctly, he was also told to start work the following week and to get a new suit.

Life as a shop assistant could be very hard. Some shops took on teenagers as apprentices and didn't pay them for the first three months or more. The working day could be up to twelve hours, with one half-day off per week, hard manual work, scrubbing floors and counters and lifting heavy loads. One woman employed in a shop in a country town recalled that she spent much of her time 'plucking turkeys, geese and chickens'. For boys, a job in menswear retail was considered good and steady. Hundreds applied to do apprenticeships in stores such as Arnott's in Dublin. 'You did your time for three years and for the first three months, your tools were a dust pan and brush.' When apprentices completed their term in Arnott's, they were usually let go, but were well qualified to get a job elsewhere.

Families could help get their children work, too. One Dublin teenager, a few months out of school, was told by his carpenter father that he was to come to work with him, and so his working life began. The broadcaster Kevin Haugh, working in his father's grocery shop in Dublin, delivered messages on his bike and served customers behind the counter. He annoyed his father by spraying the area around the counter to get rid of the flies that buzzed around the meat and fish.

The army was not a favoured choice of career for the children interviewed by Shane Leslie in 1950, but nevertheless, a large number of boys did join the military. This was particularly so towards the end of the decade when the army started a recruitment campaign, seeking 500 recruits in 1959. For example, one teenage boy abandoned his vocation to be a Christian Brother and entered military life instead. Girls could not join the army at this time, although a few would join the British military, where there were women's units.

As the 1950s ended, Irish soldiers were being prepared for deployment on United Nations peacekeeping duties. Theoretically, only soldiers of 18 or over were supposed to serve overseas, but it didn't always work out like that. There were lads who would go out to the Congo in 1960 and 1961 whose mothers were still collecting child benefit for them back in Ireland. In some photos of soldiers taken at the end of the 1950s, there are teenagers whose army caps are too big for them.

The F.C.A. (Reserve Defence Force) allowed boys as young as 14 to join. For F.C.A. boys, army life was often very enjoyable, with weekend camps, sporting opportunities, and pay as well. Other teenagers joined the British or Irish merchant navies at 15 or 16 and got to see the world. One youth from a poor area of the Midlands recalled his excitement at visiting places such as Egypt, India and Singapore before he turned 18.

Many school leavers took up apprenticeships in various trades. These apprenticeships could improve their skills and employment practices, but there were complaints about the length of some apprenticeship schemes.

It took an apprenticeship of seven years to become a plasterer or bricklayer and six years to become a carpenter or plumber. Cork VEC insisted that girls seeking to do an apprenticeship in hairdressing needed a Leaving Certificate, although this was not the case in other areas. In some cases, the first year of the apprenticeship was unpaid.

For many, however, the apprenticeship system worked out well. The singer Joe Dolan did an apprenticeship as a printer with the *Westmeath Examiner* newspaper and was always proud that he could print up a flyer or document, although he never actually worked in the job he was trained for. As the decade advanced, more and more 14- and 15-year-olds seem to have decided to improve matters for themselves, and employers began to insist that apprentices continue in some form of education or do pre-apprenticeship courses. If they were not in vocational schools by day, they went there by night, to avail of courses in bookkeeping, woodwork, carpentry and other skills. Some VEC authorities – Cork, Waterford and Limerick cities, for example – made it compulsory for 14- to 16-year-olds who were not still in full-time education to attend 180 hours of tuition per annum. The messenger boys, shop assistants, factory workers, labourers, etc. were compelled to spend at least one day a week in vocational school. The numbers of 13- to 18-year-olds getting some form of educational qualification rose steadily throughout the decade – although it should be noted that as late as 1960, only 56,000 sat the Inter Cert exam, and that there were reservations among academics and business leaders as to the worth of many of the courses on offer in the VEC sector.

Few working class children stayed in school past 14. The income they could earn in employment was often needed in the home, and they were encouraged by their parents to get a job. Most working-class girls went into factories, though many aspired to occupations such as hairdressing, cooking and dressmaking. Some apprenticeships could cost up to £25 a year, although in many cases these fees were paid by trade unions. One Cork girl who started a factory job in 1953 aged 14 explained: 'There was no one with big jobs. You were in all kinds of factory work and that was that.'

Girls' jobs were secretarial or office work, Civil Service posts, teaching, nursing, shop work and waitressing. Parents wanted their children 'to get a permanent pensionable job. That was the way to live that time.' The often very young workers were subject to close supervision by parents and employers. One girl remembered being warned against going to particular dances. Some teenagers were forced to give up their job if a parent did not like what they were working at or where they were working. Teenage girls, in particular, were sometimes summoned home to care for sick relatives or to help raise younger siblings.

For the working teenagers of the 1950s, there was money to spend on entertainment – records, clothes, nights out dancing to the music of showbands or at the cinema. But the wages were often not great – even at a time when a few pennies could go a long way. Rather than 'the bank of Mum and Dad', there was 'the bank of teenage son and daughter'. Many households were dependent on the wages contributed by teenage children, and many teenagers gave part or all of their wages to their parents. The emigrants' remittances, which helped keep Ireland going, included large contributions from teenagers. In some country areas, teenagers also provided 'important free labour, which was often essential to the financial viability of small family holdings'.

Teenagers felt a certain pride in helping to support parents and help younger siblings stay in school. As one woman said, 'All the children who went in the '40s and '50s did the same thing. They went to help the younger children and to educate them – yeah, we did, we educated them.' For at least half the teenagers who went into the workforce in the 1950s, the ultimate destination was Britain or America, Canada or Australia. A girl from Mayo noted that emigration was seen as inevitable: 'Everyone would head off with a little bag in hand because there was nothing for us in Ireland.'

For the great majority of those who emigrated, Britain was where they ended up – a country that, for much of the decade, enjoyed near full employment, and needed workers. Those with little education worked as manual labourers or as maids, waitresses or factory hands. Those with skills and an Inter Cert found work with companies such as British Rail, the car factories of Coventry, Luton or Dagenham, the mills of Yorkshire and Lancashire, or helping to build roads and power stations. The NHS gave work to countless Irish girls and young women. Teenage girls were particularly likely to emigrate once they got past their sixteenth birthday. Many had little desire to stay in small-town or rural Ireland, where job opportunities were scarce. Britain offered girls levels of freedom that were not available at home. One teenage girl in the Midlands left a post in her local council for a job at British Rail because she realised the opportunities for promotion were much better in England and she would be able to keep her job if she married. The pay was better, the chance to improve one's education through night classes or daytime courses was greater, and employers such as the NHS provided free training and even accommodation.

By the end of the 1950s, the numbers of teenagers in part- or full-time education was growing steadily, but a majority of those aged between 14 and 18 were wage earners and taxpayers, perhaps growing up faster and being more mature than the teenagers of later generations.

8

The Outsiders

For probably the majority of children in 1950s Ireland, life was reasonably happy and perhaps less pressurised than for their twenty-first-century counterparts, and they got plenty of exercise and nutritious food. They were given the freedom to play outside, to take risks and to learn to be resourceful. Drugs were not a problem and crime rates were low. But for a significant minority of children in the decade, life was hard and often very frightening. These were children who were born in mother and baby homes, the children consigned to industrial schools, the teenage girls sent to the Magdalene Laundries, or the 'backward' children for whom there was little understanding and help. The Ireland of the 1950s was a land in which astonishingly large numbers of people were incarcerated in what writer Bruce Arnold has described as 'Ireland's Gulag' – a network of asylums, mother and baby homes, prisons, industrial schools, reformatories and laundries. It was also a land with a very deep class divide, in which children became aware very early on of the unbridgeable gap separating them from other children with different addresses. There were degrees of citizenship in Ireland then, and the children of the poor were often considered to be of very little value and frequently denied their constitutional rights.

In 1950s Ireland it was very rare for a child to be born outside wedlock – the 'illegitimacy' rate was just 2.5 per cent, one of the lowest in the world. Single, 'unmarried' mothers were regarded as sinners of the darkest hue, and were frequently disowned by their families. The girls who got pregnant outside marriage were often sent to England to have the baby or to a mother and baby home in Ireland – usually one as far as possible from their home area.

In Roman Catholic dioceses in England, such as Westminster, authorities became well used to the arrival on the boat train of teenage girls or young women, who were referred to as 'PFI – Pregnant from Ireland'. The teenagers, in particular, were often completely clueless as to the facts of life. They were boarded out in homes or sent to mother and baby homes in Britain. The babies were usually put up for adoption, placed in foster care, or were kept by the mother, who stayed in Britain. These children would form a 'hidden diaspora' within British society.

The mother and baby homes in Ireland – located in places such as Tuam, Co. Galway, Dublin, Castlepollard in Westmeath and Roscrea in Tipperary, were harsh and punitive places for the (often teenage) mothers-to-be sent there. They were expected to work for their keep by the nuns who ran these establishments, and the work could include heavy manual work in the fields – picking potatoes, for instance. When the time came to give birth, painkillers were sometimes withheld. The babies were usually kept in a ward on one floor of the building, and the mothers stayed on another floor – only allowed access to their children for an hour or two at most per day. They were often pressured to give their babies up for adoption as soon as possible.

Adoption was only legalised in Ireland in 1952, but even before that, adoptions from mother and baby homes took place. There was a lucrative trade in babies to America, and Ireland gained something of a reputation as a country where couples seeking to adopt could acquire a baby with little difficulty – being a Roman Catholic and reasonably well off were the only criteria sought by many in Church and State when handing over babies to Americans who came calling. In many cases, babies were sent on falsified documents – making it almost impossible for them to find out in later years who their biological mothers were. The film *Philomena*, based on the book *The Lost Child of Philomena Lee*, gives a powerful account of one such baby adopted in America, as well as his efforts to find his mother and her efforts to find him. Babies and children were sometimes advertised for adoption in the national newspapers.

Not all babies were adopted, however. Generally only the fair and pretty ones were wanted. Most of the babies spent the entire day in their cots, sometimes being looked after by teenage girls from industrial schools who were usually unqualified to care for them, though they tried their best. A number of these babies ended up in industrial schools; others were fostered out to families.

Some teenage girls found themselves committed to Magdalene Laundries. Occasionally this was for petty theft, but it could also be because they were pregnant outside wedlock or considered to be in 'moral danger'. These laundries, in places such as Sean McDermott Street in Dublin, went back to the eighteenth century, but were still full in the 1950s. Like the mother and baby homes, they were run by religious orders such as the Mercy Nuns and the Sisters of Charity. The 'Maggies', as they were known, toiled long hours in the laundries in poor working conditions and under strict discipline, doing laundry for businesses and even for government departments and the military. Being sent to a Magdalene Laundry was not a life sentence, but many girls became institutionalised, or had nowhere else to go and so stayed, providing Church and State with what amounted to a slave labour workforce. The hard physical work in the laundry damaged their health and girls frequently fainted in the extreme heat and often suffered injury from heavy machinery.

There were more than fifty industrial schools in Ireland in the 1950s – stretching from Cavan to Tralee and from Dublin to Letterfrack. At the start of the decade there were up to 6,000 children incarcerated in these schools. The schools were nearly all run by Roman Catholic religious orders such as the Sisters of Charity, the Mercy Nuns and the Oblate Fathers. There were also industrial schools connected to Protestant churches.

The majority of children in industrial schools came from households where one parent was dead or there was considerable poverty, bordering on destitution. Quite a number of the children were 'illegitimate'. Children were sent to the schools by the courts, or by local authorities keen to save money that would otherwise have to be spent on their upkeep, or by desperate parents unable for one reason or another to care for them.

Children were brought before courts, where they were referred to as 'the defendant' and were rarely spoken to about their problems or their wishes. Children as young as 2 years old sat in courtrooms, where they were described as being destitute or illegitimate. The courts sent them to the industrial schools, where they were to be detained until the day before they turned 16. Many children spent longer imprisoned in industrial schools than serious criminals spent in jail. Their detention in these schools was actually against the law of the land and the constitution, but was rarely challenged. The industrial schools were, in fact, child prisons, although those imprisoned had rarely committed anything but the most minor offence.

Those running the industrial schools were paid a capitation grant by the State for each child, and sometimes money was taken from parents as well. The religious orders would later claim that the State paid them too little to care for the children, but in fact the schools made a profit for those running them because the children provided an unpaid workforce. At schools such as Artane in Dublin, the inmates worked long hours in the fields and in workshops producing goods for sale. One newspaper headline in the 1950s declared that 'they make everything in Artane'. At one industrial school, a profit of £100,000 was made in one year from the provision of goods and services, including laundry services, to the local town. The children who did the work received no payment at all from that profit.

In many of the schools, minimal education was provided. Boys and girls left the so-called schools after a decade or more all but illiterate. In some schools such as Letterfrack and Artane, the children were trained in trades such as carpentry or tailoring, but in a lot of the schools they learned nothing at all.

The cruelty inflicted on thousands of incarcerated children in 1950s Ireland by priests, nuns, brothers and lay staff was horrific. Children were beaten daily with belts and canes, punched and kicked. They were locked in dark cupboards for hours at a time, thrown into scalding water, or left outside in the freezing cold. While some inmates were fed reasonably well, others were virtually starved. In 1955, a senior official from the Department of Education reported that in Daingean Reformatory, the cows were better looked after than the boys. The sexual abuse of children was widespread and the treatment of some children amounted to torture. A number of children died in mysterious circumstances. Documents relating to the children such as birth and death certificates often disappeared or were altered. In one mother and baby home, St Joseph's Industrial School near Tuam, it has emerged that babies who died there were dumped in septic tanks.

Survivors of one industrial school remembered how, having heard that other children got presents at Christmas from Santa Claus, they hung up stockings on Christmas Eve, but on Christmas morning the stockings were empty: 'Santa never came to us.' Children were occasionally given toys at Christmas, but the toys would be taken away from them after a few hours or days. In most cases birthdays were never celebrated, with the children often having no idea when their actual birthday was. The children were robbed of their individuality and their identity – given new names and often referred to by the numbers that were sewn on their clothes and shoes.

Industrial school children were set to work from a very young age, sometimes as young as 6. They scrubbed floors, polished, toiled on farms and did the laundry for the nuns, as well as for the middle class students of the fee-paying schools that were sometimes located right beside industrial schools and run by the same religious orders. In the age before washing machines, religious orders made profits offering laundry services to the towns in which the schools were located. There was a demand for their services and a large unpaid workforce to provide it.

The children in the schools were not completely isolated from the world around them, however. They were brought out for walks under the ever-watchful supervision of the nuns or brothers. In Dun Laoghaire, people could hear the clumping of the hobnail boots worn by the children before they saw them marching along in military precision. People noticed how thin and pale the children from the schools were, and how unnaturally subdued they seemed to be. At Croke Park, during All-Ireland Finals, the Artane Boys' Band entertained the fans and players with great style and ability, but when the children were not playing they were corralled away in one area of the stadium under the eyes of the brothers and were pathetically grateful for any sweets, toys or fruit thrown at them by their audience.

Occasionally, children would be given a week's summer holiday with a family who would volunteer to take them in. For that week they would be properly fed and cared for, then returned to their prison.

The law was occasionally challenged. In 1955, Dublin man Desmond Doyle successfully managed to get his daughter Evelyn out of the industrial school to which she had been sent after her mother left the family home and moved to England. The court ruled in favour of Mr Doyle's parental rights over his children. The school in which Evelyn Doyle was detained was better than most, in that she was treated kindly by some of the nuns and was properly fed, clothed and educated. But for too many children in the 1950s, childhood was the stuff of nightmares because of the actions of Church and State. The whole system of industrial schools, laundries and mother and baby homes has cast a long shadow over Irish history. The number of children sent to industrial schools declined in the later 1950s, in part because courts were increasingly reluctant to send children to them, but the scandal of Ireland's child prisons would continue for more than a decade after the end of the 1950s.

Poverty was still widespread in Ireland sixty years ago. For much of the decade, the country was one of the poorest in Western Europe (only Portugal was worse). This poverty was the main reason the country had such a shockingly high infant mortality rate as the decade began. The poverty in which so many children lived was visible to many. The children of the poor, in areas such as north inner-city Dublin, looked thin, had bad teeth and were completely lacking in any kind of self-confidence, often appearing hunched as they walked along. Illnesses such as TB still stalked the poor until the middle of the decade. In school, their clothes were often ragged, their legs chapped from wearing wellingtons without socks and their fingers very badly chilblained.

In a society deeply divided by social class, the children of the poor were often relegated to the back of the class. Many who were children at that time recall that how one was treated by teachers seemed to depend on who your parents were and from which part of town they